SEXUAL ADDICTION

SEXUAL ADDICTION
Psychoanalytic Concepts and the Art of Supervision

Vamık D. Volkan

PHOENIX
PUBLISHING HOUSE
firing the mind

First published in 2021 by
Phoenix Publishing House Ltd
62 Bucknell Road
Bicester
Oxfordshire OX26 2DS

British Library Cataloguing in Publication Data

A C.I.P. for this book is available from the British Library

ISBN-13: 978-1-912691-38-8

Typeset by vPrompt eServices Pvt Ltd, India

Printed in the United Kingdom

www.firingthemind.com

With fond memories and admiration this book is dedicated to those I taught and supervised throughout my career

Contents

About the author

Vamık D. Volkan is an emeritus professor of psychiatry at the University of Virginia, an emeritus training and supervising analyst at the Washington-Baltimore Psychoanalytic Institute and an emeritus Senior Erik Erikson Scholar at the Erikson Institute of the Austen Riggs Center, Stockbridge, Massachusetts. He is the emeritus president of the International Dialogue Initiative and a former president of the Turkish-American Neuropsychiatric Society, the International Society of Political Psychology, the Virginia Psychoanalytic Society, and the American College of Psychoanalysts.

Dr. Volkan was the founder and the director of the Center for the Study of Mind and Human Interaction (CSMHI) at the School of Medicine, University of Virginia. CSMHI applied a growing theoretical and field-proven base of knowledge to issues such as ethnic tension, racism, terrorism, societal trauma, immigration, mourning, trans-generational transmissions and leader–follower relationships. CSMHI conducted years-long unofficial diplomatic dialogues between Americans and Soviets, Russians and prominent representatives in the Baltic States, Croats and Bosniaks, Georgians and South Ossetians, Turks and Greeks, and studied post-revolution or post-war societies such as Albania and

Romania after the time of dictators Enver Hoxha and Nicolae Ceauşescu and Kuwait after the Iraqi invasion.

Dr. Volkan was a member of the International Negotiation Network (INN) under the directorship of former President Jimmy Carter; a temporary consultant to the World Health Organization in Albania and Macedonia; a member of the International Advisory Board, Leonard Davis Institute for International Relations, Hebrew University, Jerusalem, Israel; an inaugural Yitzhak Rabin Fellow, Rabin Center for Israeli Studies, Tel Aviv, Israel; a visiting professor of psychiatry, University of Ankara in the Turkish capital, Ege University in Izmir and Cerrahpaşa Medical School in Istanbul, Turkey; a visiting professor of political psychology, Bahceşehir University, Istanbul, Turkey; an honorary supervisor and consultant, Società per lo studio dei disturbi della personalità in Milan, Italy; a visiting professor of law, Harvard University, Boston, Massachusetts; a Fulbright/Sigmund Freud-Foundation visiting scholar of psychoanalysis in Vienna, Austria; a visiting professor of political science at the University of Vienna; a board member of the Freud Foundation in Vienna; a member of the Working Group on Terror and Terrorism, International Psychoanalytical Association, and a visiting professor at El Bosque University, Bogota, Colombia.

Dr. Volkan is a recipient of the Nevitt Sanford, Elise Hayman, Bryce Boyer, Hans Strupp, Sigmund Freud (given by the city of Vienna), and Mary Sigourney awards and the Margaret Mahler Literature Prize. He was nominated for the Nobel Peace Prize five times; letters of support were sent from twenty-seven countries. Dr. Volkan holds honorary doctorate degrees from Kuopio University (now called the University of Eastern Finland), Finland; Ankara University, Turkey; the Eastern European Psychoanalytic Institute, Russia; Eastern Mediterranean University, North Cyprus; and Kyrenia-American University, North Cyprus.

Dr. Volkan is the author, coauthor, editor, or coeditor of sixty psycho-analytic and psycho-political books, some of which have been translated into Chinese, Finnish, German, Greek, Japanese, Russian, Serbian, Spanish, and Turkish. He has written hundreds of published papers and book chapters and has served on the editorial boards of sixteen national or international professional journals.

About this book

In 2002, I retired from my position as a member of the Department of Psychiatry at the University of Virginia in Charlottesville, Virginia after thirty-eight years. Over a decade later, I received a call from Dr. Rowan. I remembered him as a young physician when he was doing his psychiatric residency at the university. At that time, due to my administrative duties, I was not supervising psychiatric residents' cases, but Dr. Rowan had been present when I gave a few lectures for the trainees. When he called me I learned that, following the completion of his residency training, he, his wife, and their little son had moved far away from Charlottesville to a big city where he opened an office and started a private psychiatric practice. Later he became a candidate at a psychoanalytic institute, but had not yet graduated. He was asking me to supervise his therapeutic work with a difficult patient, Judy.

Judy was an attractive, thirty-year-old, single woman when she became Dr. Rowan's psychotherapy patient. She held a respectable position at a big business firm with international branches. She was in charge of developing strategies for maintaining and improving her firm's investments in other countries and often traveled internationally. Her French was perfect. She had lived in Paris for over two years before returning to the United States and settling in the city where her firm's headquarters and Dr. Rowan's office were located. She was living alone in her own apartment.

Judy was aware that she had been feeling very lonely in spite of her busy schedule and responsibilities at work and her ability to appear as a very social individual. While at university, she had the same boyfriend for over two years but since then, she frequented nightclubs or bars to "hunt" men for sex. She called herself a "hunter." She would hunt constantly, at least a few times a month and often a few times a week. When having sex with these men, sometimes she would reach orgasm and other times she would not. Occasionally, she stayed with the same man for a short time, a week or a month, and sometimes she would keep in touch with a few of them over a year or two. But her obligatory habit was to "hunt" different sex partners for one-night stands. Once she caught a virus while hunting. Fortunately, her medical treatment was successful. She knew that she had to stop her sex habit, but she was aware that she could not.

When she faced the possibility of catching a new infection, which in reality did not happen, Judy decided to seek help from Dr. Rowan. Soon after meeting her, he noticed that when describing her experiences of one-night stands with strangers, Judy would always use the term "lovemaking." He sensed that Judy's "hunting" experiences were connected with her wish to collect "love."

In this book I will describe in detail Judy's psychoanalytic treatment during its first three years, the time span during which I was Dr. Rowan's supervisor. Then I will tell what happened to Judy later, from information kindly provided to me by Dr. Rowan. This is not the first time I have written about the psychoanalytic process using case studies in this way. To understand why I believe this to be a valuable exercise, a bit of history is useful.

In 1953, Anna Freud, with then well-known psychoanalysts Edith Jacobson, Edith Weigert, and Leo Stone, discussed the "widening scope of psychoanalysis." During this discussion she asked, "How do analysts decide if they are given the choice between returning to health half a dozen young people with good prospects in life but disturbed in their enjoyment and efficiency by comparatively mild neuroses, or to devote the same time, trouble and effort to one single borderline case, who may or may not be saved from spending the rest of his life in an institution?"

(A. Freud, 1954, pp. 610–611). Anna Freud's bias was toward treating *only* neurotic patients instead of struggling with new technical problems. This type of attitude could not be maintained.

As time went on, with the influence of new theories, new "schools," and other factors, such as economic ones, psychoanalysts began to treat individuals with narcissistic and borderline personality organizations, as well as individuals with extreme traumatic childhood histories. But generally speaking, people with addictions, especially with chemical addictions, still did not have access to psychoanalytic couches.

Since Sigmund Freud's time there have always been different psychoanalytic "schools." Robert Wallerstein, during his presidential address to the 35th International Psychoanalytical Association Congress, expressed concern about the competition among new psychoanalytic theories and trends and asked the question of whether we would have one psychoanalysis or many (Wallerstein, 1988). In 2002, Leo Rangell, once president of the International Psychoanalytical Association and twice president of the American Psychoanalytic Association, also expressed concern about a "growth of pluralism" (p. 1118) in psychoanalysis. He considered the structural view (the ego, id, and superego) to be the apex of psychoanalytic theory. "Without it," he said, "much of the power of psychoanalytic theory is lost" (p. 1131). He added: "No explanation of the ubiquitous unconscious intrapsychic process, with its ongoing scanning for safety or anxiety, and its myriad psychic outcomes, from normal to pathological, is possible without the structural view" (p. 1131). In 2006 Arnold Cooper edited a book in which he and the other contributors wondered if we were witnessing "new wine in old bottles or the hidden revolution in psychoanalysis" (p. 51). Different ways of listening to the patient and different styles of handling clinical material started a pointless struggle and began to put analysts in rather different professions. The following questions were raised: What is psychoanalytic treatment? Who is a psychoanalyst? Who can benefit from being on a psychoanalyst's couch? (Böhm, 2002; Green, 2000; Kernberg, 2001).

Following these developments in psychoanalysis, I turned my attention to the benefits and pitfalls of this new growth of pluralism and wrote a textbook that includes new ideas for psychoanalytic technique (Volkan, 2010a). I stated that questioning some classic assumptions and introducing new ways of understanding human psychology is an enriching process. I also noted that the new "growth of pluralism" has supported resistances against examining some unconscious material in depth. Since individuals with different personality organizations lie on psychoanalysts' couches, I also noted that there was a need to consider specific technical approaches for analysands according to their having a neurotic, narcissistic, borderline, or psychotic personality organization.

Besides writing a textbook, I began providing psychoanalytic case examples spanning the first to the last days of analysis and reported what comes to the analyst's mind—and when cases were supervised, also the supervisor's mind—as the analytic process continued (Volkan, 2009, 2010a, 2010b, 2010c, 2012, 2014, 2015, 2019; Volkan & Fowler, 2009). Writing total case histories allows the reader to question the validity of the link between clinical observations, the psychodynamic understanding of them, and technical considerations based on such observations. It is very difficult to measure scientifically the outcome of psychoanalytic treatment because psychoanalysts deal with unconscious elements. The best way to describe changes in a person's internal world, I believe, is to recount total psychoanalytic processes without hiding behind psychoanalytic theoretical terms and without becoming a spokesperson for a specific psychoanalytic "school."

In writing this book I had the following *four aims* in my mind:

My first aim in writing this book is to provide another example of a total psychoanalytic process, this time illustrating issues in analyzing, as well as supervising, a case of one who was trying to solve her early life's deprivations through remembering her deprived childhood self-image and wished-for love-object through actions, including a non-chemical addiction.

My second aim is to provide an understanding of the psychology of addiction, a non-chemical one. Judy was suffering from "sexual addiction." In Chapter 2 I review the psychoanalytic literature on chemical and non-chemical addictions starting with Sigmund Freud's remarks about this topic in 1897. During my long career as a psychiatrist and a psychoanalyst, I did not treat a person with chemical addiction and never supervised a younger colleague working with such a case. Psychoanalysts, in general, do not work intensively with patients with chemical addiction. In 2009, Christopher Fowler and I published a book. In it I described the case of a man who started his analysis me when he was fifty-seven years old stating that he was suffering from "sexual addiction." As a child in the American South, he had "multiple mothers": his biological mother, his paternal grandmother, and his black nanny. As an adult he could not reconcile his seemingly opposite mothering experiences. He was searching for a "perfect woman" (Volkan & Fowler, 2009). I also supervised the case of Herman who engaged in compulsive masturbation and whose case I will describe in Chapter 3.

My third aim is to illustrate some therapeutic concepts and issues. From the beginning of her analysis and through her treatment, Judy's case made me pay attention to certain *therapeutic concepts and issues.* Here is a list of them:

- Built-in transference
- Twinning
- Linking interpretation
- Preparatory interpretation
- The first dream
- Reaching-up
- Animals on the couch
- Hoarding
- Externalization, internalization
- Acting out, acting in, second look, pilgrimage, enactment
- Therapeutic play
- New object (analytic introject) (developmental object)
- Multiple mothers
- Crucial juncture experience
- Psychoanalytic neutrality
- Rebirth fantasy, new beginning
- Covid-19 and psychoanalysis.

I will describe these concepts and issues by referring to Judy's case, but also to the cases of Alex, Herman, Samantha, Rebecca, Jennifer, Pattie, Peter, and others. I will provide historical background, often going back to Sigmund Freud's writings, for such concepts and issues to illustrate how they appeared in the psychoanalytic literature.

We may not focus on such concepts or see some of these issues while working with routine cases with neurotic personalities. But without paying attention to them, we miss understanding the internal worlds of other patients with preoedipal deprivations, conflicts, and fixations and finding ways for analyzing them.

My fourth aim is to share my thoughts and feelings about working with Dr. Rowan and how I handled them as a supervisor. The topic of the psychoanalytic supervisor–supervisee relationship and the supervisor's emotional reactions toward the analysand whom the supervisor never meets are, generally speaking, rather ignored in the psychoanalytic literature. The most recent extensive look at the supervisory experience appears in the 2019 special issue of the *American Journal of Psychoanalysis* and includes contributors' theoretical and practical conclusions on supervisors' and supervisees' communications and responses. Hanoch Yerushalmi (2019), the guest editor of this special issue, brings to our attention the influence of the "analytic community" to which the supervisor belongs in conducting supervision (see also Frawley-O'Dea & Sarnat, 2001). For Yerushalmi, the concept of analytic community "refers to a group of professionals serving as a cultural-professional framework for each other's therapeutic and supervisory interactions" (p. 257). He notes that the analytic community's core beliefs and perceptions have remained basically unchanged during the many years of its existence outside of some alterations and adaptation to new concepts.

In my book *Ghosts in the Human Psyche: The Story of a "Muslim Armenian"* (Volkan, 2019), I refer to the impact of past and present historical events, cultural elements, political movements, and their mental images on the psyche of individuals; and my need, as a supervisor, to bring these issues to my supervisee's attention. Judy's case presented *unusual actions* by the analysand, and supervision included a careful focus on the analyst's keeping his therapeutic neutrality and developing his psychoanalytic identity. I hope that a close look at a supervisor–supervisee relationship will create more interest in studying this topic, especially in present-day psychoanalysis with its different "schools."

I keep extensive notes while I supervise a younger colleague's work. I will tell the story of Judy's first three years of psychoanalysis by referring to them. As I stated earlier, Dr. Rowan stopped receiving supervision from me for Judy's analysis after three years.

In order to protect Judy's and her analyst's real identities, I have made some changes in my descriptions of their *external lives* with the belief that none of these changes interferes with my illustration of Judy's internal world and her analyst's response to my supervision and work with Judy.

CHAPTER 1

A "hunter" of men

When he called me, Dr. Rowan had been seeing Judy face to face once a week in psychotherapy for two years. He had considerable information about her background and ideas related to the causes of her hunting behavior. He told me that his patient's not having a "good enough mother" (Winnicott, 1971), a mother who was unable to have a full adaptation for her baby's or child's psychological needs, was the main factor in her constant search for a libidinal object via her "hunting" addiction. But Dr. Rowan was frustrated by Judy's stubborn resistance against remaining curious about the possible psychological determinants of her lifestyle. He was noticing "no workable transference" development.

Judy would fill her sessions with details of her hunting and having sex with different men and her traveling to other countries as part of her profession, jumping from one topic to another. Dr. Rowan began to experience boredom and frustration while Judy was in his office. He also became aware that he was joining his patient in her preoccupation with her daily activities by asking her questions, such as who were the men she met recently, why she chose one over another, why she did not think more carefully about protecting herself from getting pregnant or catching a virus, how was she getting along with her coworkers, and how her recent overseas trip had gone. Judy's psychotherapy would sometimes turn into a "question and answer" session.

One day while sitting in front of Judy and experiencing boredom, Dr. Rowan remembered his days in Charlottesville as a psychiatric resident. When he thought of asking Judy a question, he recalled that during one of my lectures I gave the details of a teaching program I had at the University of Virginia for psychiatric residents before he came to Charlottesville. At that time, psychiatric patients, unlike today, could stay as inpatients at a university hospital for a long time, for many months, even over a year. My teaching program was designed to encourage residents to "walk together" with their patients, side by side, and be curious together about what they were seeing rather than machine-gunning their patients with questions.

A resident would meet a new inpatient in a room while a group of residents and I would watch and hear them in another room behind a one-way mirror. We would ask the resident sitting with the patient to get a detailed history of the patient's developmental years and conduct the psychotherapy sessions *without* asking any questions, or at least without asking *many* questions. The patient, who was seen in this setting for every therapeutic session, was observed by the group only twice weekly. When not observed, the therapist provided a detailed account of the interview at the next group meeting. The dynamics of the group itself were put to use in elucidating psychodynamic principles (Volkan & Hawkins, 1971a, 1971b).

Recalling my lecture, Dr. Rowan decided to call me and ask if I would agree to be his supervisor. I stated that if Judy would be willing to lie on his couch four times a week, I would consider working with him. He thought that since psychotherapy was not helping Judy, he would go along with me. When I felt reassured that my becoming Dr. Rowan's supervisor for Judy's psychoanalytic process would not any way interfere with his official training at his psychoanalytic institute, I agreed to work with him. Judy agreed to lie on Dr. Rowan's couch four times a week and cut down on her future traveling schedule.

Since the late 1990s I have provided supervision and consultation for younger analysts who lived a ways from my home and in different countries. I started to supervise Dr. Rowan from a distance by telephone.

We also agreed to meet in person once a year when both of us attended a professional meeting.

Franco De Masi (2019) writes that, "The kind of environmental response that the person received during the first part of his life lays the foundations for his later emotional disposition" (p. 391). Accordingly, in supervisions, he firmly insists upon this so that the supervisee "can comprehend how the patient engages in the therapeutic task and with his analyst" (p. 391). Like De Masi, when I begin supervising a new case I bring to the analyst's attention the importance of the patient's personal history, especially that of childhood. Since he had seen Judy in psychotherapy for two years, Dr. Rowan gave me detailed information about her life history.

As she was growing up, Judy perceived her mother as an intelligent woman who was constantly searching for love. Judy knew that her own main adult personality characteristic was similar to her mother's. Dr. Rowan already had ideas about why Judy's mother was hungry for love. She had two older brothers and when she was a baby, her second brother died of an illness. Judy's maternal grandmother became depressed and did not provide adequate mothering for her daughter. Judy's maternal grandfather was a physician, and the family was comfortable economically. They were interested in intellectual activities, but it appears that psychological poisons due to the loss of their preadolescent son remained in the family members' minds. When Judy's mother was in her early twenties, her other brother was taken to a mental hospital where he later committed suicide.

Judy was the second child; she had a brother two years older. When she was a child, Judy's father's profession often kept him away from home for days or even weeks. Sometimes the whole family had to relocate to isolated locations both in the United States and in foreign lands where they had no relatives or friends. This situation made for great loneliness, as Judy's mother, as well as her son and daughter, searched for normal everyday relationships.

Judy called her childhood father "despotic." She had memories of him hitting her while her mother tried to protect her. However, she remembered her mother also physically hurting her and her brother. Sometimes her mother would punish little Judy by not allowing her to eat and making her experience *hunger*. Judy also sensed that her mother preferred her brother over her.

Judy remembered playing with a cousin when she was five or six years old. One day this cousin, who was nine or ten years older than she, molested her. All she could recall was that he touched her genital area and made her handle his penis. She could not describe other details of this molestation. But she said that as an adult, being a molested child as well as being an unwanted child often came to her mind.

Judy's maternal grandmother died when Judy was nine years old. One month later her mother told Judy, "You are going to have another sibling." Judy remembered her mother taking her to a shopping center where the mother bought maternity clothes. Later, Judy's mother went through an ultrasound examination and her physician told her that she might be carrying a fetus with some physical problems. The mother showed the ultrasound film to her daughter, and Judy still recalled seeing her new sibling like a dot on the film. The physician connected the fetus' condition to some medications Judy's mother was taking. Judy's mother had an abortion and became depressed. It is most probable that the mother linked her new loss to her childhood experience of losing a brother, later losing another sibling, and most recently losing her mother. One thing is clear: during the preoedipal phase of her life and her early teen years, Judy was hungry for maternal care and love.

When Judy was eleven years old, and she and her family were on a summer vacation, a sixteen-year-old boy asked her to go out with him. She was puzzled and said "no." When her father learned about this teenager's interest in his daughter, he screamed at Judy, "You cannot go out with a boy until I say you can." As a teenager Judy avoided dating boys. As I stated earlier, while attending university, she had the same boyfriend for over two years, her only long-term experience with a man. Since then, Judy had no lasting relationships and she had become a "hunter of men."

While working with Dr. Rowan, Judy also became aware that, as an adult, she was doing something similar to what her father did during her childhood: She was traveling often to different locations in the US and to foreign countries as part of her own profession. She wondered if she was identifying with her father. Dr. Rowan wondered if this identification might be another expression of Judy's searching for someone who might care for her. This time her father, whose image, however, was a scary despotic one. This would create complications for Judy's reaching up to her father.

While Judy was Dr. Rowan's patient, her father and mother lived in another city. Her father was retired, and he and Judy's mother would frequently take vacations. On some occasions Judy would purchase their travel tickets as gifts. The communication between Judy and her parents took place primarily through telephone conversations. According to Judy, her parents had no idea about her hypersexuality. On the other hand, Judy had a very special relationship with her brother.

From early childhood on, Judy would seek physical closeness with her brother and share her feelings of loneliness. During the time Judy saw Dr. Rowan in psychotherapy, her brother and his wife were newly married and soon had a son. They lived in the city where Judy was located, but in a district distant from her place. Before he was married Judy would call her brother almost daily and present details of her "hunting" and sexual activities. She was absolutely sure that her brother would keep her secrets. She continued to do so after her brother became a married man, while his wife was pregnant, and after their son was born.

There are different kinds of sexual addictions. For example, some persons' masturbation activities or others' pedophilia are referred to as addictions. Judy had a sexual hunting addiction. In the next chapter, I will review psychoanalytic observations and thoughts on addictions, including non-chemical ones.

CHAPTER 2

Psychoanalytic perspectives on addictions

In a letter to Wilhelm Fliess written in 1897 Sigmund Freud states: "It has dawned on me that masturbation is the one major habit, the 'primal addiction' and that it is only as a substitute and replacement for it that the other addictions—for alcohol, morphine, tobacco, etc.— come to existence" (p. 272). The next year he concluded that "the most immediate and, for practical purposes, the most significant causes of every case of neurotic illness are to be found in factors arising from sexual life" (1898a, p. 263). He briefly mentioned that successfully breaking an individual's habit of masturbation or addiction to narcotics could not be achieved without investigating the source from which the patients' imperative need for addiction springs. He stated that "'Habit' is a mere form of words, without any explanatory value" (p. 276). Freud added that when something causes depression in a former masturbator he returns to masturbation and that narcotics are substitutes for a lack of sexual satisfaction. At the time he was writing this paper he noted that psychoanalytic therapy was not applicable to all cases.

After a long interval, in 1928, Freud returned to the phenomenon of addiction by referring to Fyodor Mikhailovich Dostoevsky's addiction to gambling. He wrote: "If the addiction to gambling, with the unsuccessful struggles to break the habit and the opportunities it affords for self-punishment, is a repetition of the compulsion to masturbate, we shall not be surprised to find that it occupied such a large space in Dostoevsky's life" (1928b, p. 194). He referred to his classical psycho-analytic ideas and stated that "we find no cases of severe neurosis in which the auto-erotic satisfaction of early childhood and of puberty has not played a part; and the relation between efforts to suppress it and fear of the father are too well known to need more than a mention" (p. 194). Beyond referring to masturbation, Freud did not study sexual addictions such as Judy's. The topic of addiction was not a preoccupation for Freud.

In 1945 Otto Fenichel, in his book *The Psychoanalytic Theory of Neurosis*, provided a rich review of classical psychoanalytic theories and their clinical applications and did not ignore writing about addictions. Besides presenting his own ideas on addiction, he made references to findings by Freud's early followers. He stated that drug addiction becomes complicated due to the chemical effects of the drugs. However, "the origin and nature of the addiction are not determined by the chemical effect of the drug but by the psychological structure of the patient" (p. 376). People who are addicted to alcohol, morphine, or other drugs are trying to satisfy their sexual longing, a need for security, and a need for the maintenance of self-esteem. Fenichel also examined addictions without drugs, such as masturbation, food, reading, gambling, theft, and love. He wrote, "In some sexual activities, the sexual partner serves the same purpose as the drug in the addiction" (p. 385).

Fenichel's description of Don Juan's, as well as one of his female patient's, behavior patterns is similar to Judy's pattern of "hunting" for men. Fenichel agrees that if we consider that Don Juan's having sex with many different female partners is related to his seeking his mother without finding her, it would be obvious to think of the role of the Oedipus complex in his habit. Fenichel tells us that the analysis of Don Juan types shows that "their Oedipus complex is of a particular type. It is dominated by the pregenital aim of incorporation, pervaded by narcissistic needs and tinged with sadistic impulses" (p. 243). Such individuals strive to obtain narcissistic supplies and may develop sadistic reactions if they are not immediately satisfied. Fenichel reminds us that Don Juan, after having sex with a woman, was no longer interested in her. He would imagine that another woman might give him satisfaction.

Fenichel tells the story of a woman who had frequent intercourse with various men. She, like Judy, was a seducer. When this patient was a child, her mother's severity had frustrated her and precipitated intense oral-sadistic wishes. Then she became ill. Fenichel does not report at what age her illness started and does not give its medical diagnosis, but he writes that his patient's sickness in her childhood lasted for a long time and she experienced fear of death. In her adolescence this patient would visit cemeteries and sit on graves for hours, daydreaming and imagining the dead as peaceful.

Fenichel summarizes his understanding of his patient's internal world in the following way. His patient's mother's severity before her daughter experienced a long childhood illness had induced intense oral-sadistic wishes in this patient's mind. But during her illness the patient's mother was devoted to her and alleviated the little girl's fear of death. As an adult, whenever she seduced a man, this patient would try to be nice to him as her mother had been nice to her during her long childhood illness. During her analysis, Fenichel noted that his patient considered her sickness to have been a punishment for the aggressive feelings she felt in childhood. Thus, her kind behavior toward the men she had seduced was a defense against aggressiveness as well as fear of retaliation.

Further analysis illustrated that Fenichel's patient's tenderness was directed toward the penis. Fenichel wrote: "The men toward whom she behaved tenderly were selected on the basis of narcissistic object choice, so that she might treat them as she wanted to be treated by her mother; basically it was the penis of these men with which she had identified herself" (p. 517). Later in this book I will describe how Judy used her vagina as a mouth. Having a penis in her vagina represented taking in the needed maternal care.

Psychoanalytic papers published after 1945 showed that various types of addictions are related to oral dependency issues. Through addiction, internal narcissistic mortification is denied and replaced by external narcissistic mortification, such as "I depend on the drug" (Eidelberg, 1954, p. 210). Meanwhile, new pluralism in psychoanalysis, which I mentioned earlier, was taking place. The primary change, as André Green (2000) stated, was the focus on the role of object and the relationship between drive and object, the latter being unduly neglected in classical Freudian theory. This change led to looking at the causes of addiction from other theoretical considerations besides classical psychoanalytic points of view.

In his book *Dancing among the Maenads: The Psychology of Compulsive Drug Use*, Kevin Volkan (1994) reviewed the major tenets of classical analysis in compulsive drug use, but also added to our understanding of this subject from an object relations approach. He presented cases including those obtained from reports and suppositions found in the media concerning drug-addicted folk heroes and mythological drug users. His book made a strong case for questioning the then-existing popular emphasis on the biology of drug use. Kevin Volkan concluded that healthy early childhood object relations would play a key role in preventing individuals from becoming drug addicts. On the other hand, poor early object relations would provide grounds for risk of addiction.

After mentioning what Freud had written about addiction, John R. Giugliano (2003) reviewed the papers on addiction written in the service of the ego. In ego psychology, addiction reflects the ego's attempt to defend against primitive, sadistic impulses and intolerable affects. Giugliano referred to attachment theory (Bowlby, 1977) and stated that when individuals have weak parental attachment, they are more involved in addictions, including unrestricted sexuality. He noted how followers of object relations theories focus on the preoedipal period of separation–individuation (Mahler, 1968) and suggested that sexual addiction is understood as a failure to achieve self- and other (object) differentiation and in the service of maintaining a state of pseudo-independence. Giugliano also referred to self-psychology and described Heinz Kohut's (1977a, 1977b) insights into addiction as a regression to or fixation on the archaic nuclear self. The sexual addiction increases the self-esteem of a person with such a regression or fixation and reduces anxiety. Lastly, Giugliano brought to our attention that some sexual addictions can be related to the repetition of some childhood traumas, especially sexual ones, in adulthood.

In 2009 Salman Akhtar, in his *Comprehensive Dictionary of Psychoanalysis*, also made references to psychoanalytic writers who examined addiction from different theoretical perspectives from the drive theory, ego psychology, and self-psychology points of views. He noted that while not ignoring the role of oedipal factors, almost all the authors came to the conclusion that addiction is related to early, preoedipal damage to the personality. Later he, with Nina Savelle-Rocklin (Savelle-Rocklin & Akhtar 2019), expanded our knowledge beyond primary addiction and also, interestingly, brought to our attention a new type of addiction, addiction to the internet. In Turkey, Sercan Mansuroğlu and Hatice Tambağ (2019) reached the conclusion that internet addiction in adolescents develops a tendency toward violence in young people.

Salman Akhtar reminds us that "not all individuals with preoedipal ego damage develop addictions" (2009, p. 5) because of the role of social variables and constitutional vulnerabilities. In describing Judy's case, I will focus on the role of inefficiency of maternal care and love and, as Kevin Volkan (1994) focused on, early poor object relations. Like Salman Akhtar I also wish to remind the reader that not every person with such a background develops addictions.

I am not an expert on genetic biological factors in directing a person toward addictions. However, before returning to Judy's case, it is important to mention that scientific findings of recent decades illustrate how genetic factors become intertwined with experiences in leading to different activity patterns. How we sense the external world and behaviorally respond to it requires the function of interconnected neural circuits in the brain. Sensory neurons detect external cues and relay these activation patterns to other neurons within a neural circuit in the brain through connections much like electrical wires connected to one another. This process of sensation to action is not only dictated by how neural circuits are activated in response to environment, but is also controlled by genes that facilitate how each neuron within a neural circuit functions. It is also widely accepted that sensory and social experiences early in life have long-lasting effects on behaviors, by modifying the structure and function of neural circuits. Many circuits and behaviors are constrained by critical periods when they rely heavily on sensory experience early in life for maturation.

Studies in past decades have shown that early exposure to, or lack of, environmental cues (i.e. social experience versus social isolation) can influence behaviors by modifying how much a gene product will be made, thereby determining neural circuit function. For example, maternal tactile caring early in life modulates the levels of stress hormone receptors affecting neural circuit responses to stress and execution of anxiety-like behaviors later in life (Bagot et al., 2012; McGowan et al.,

2009; Weaver et al., 2004). In addition, the critical period for social-reward learning in adult mice requires both neural activity and bonding hormones like oxytocin (Nardou et al., 2019). These studies highlight the crucial interplay between experience, genes, neural circuit function, and behaviors.

The detailed mechanisms of how experience can affect genes and neural circuit function to modify behaviors were recently demonstrated in fruit flies. Fruit flies, like humans, have to tightly control social behaviors based on signals such as age, reproductive state, and population density to determine when and where to make a move on a mate (Sethi et al., 2019). If a male fruit fly is raised alone and is deprived of the odors of other flies, in a sense like Judy was deprived of parental care, his future mating options may be slim, and he is more likely to lose a girl fruit fly to another male.

Recently, Pelin Volkan, a biologist and the head of the Laboratory of Neurogenetics at Duke University in Durham, North Carolina, and her colleagues have demonstrated that signals from internal hormones and social experience, in the form of scent of other flies, can modify the expression of genes that govern male reproductive behaviors in fruit flies to account for these behavioral outcomes (Zhao et al., 2020). Pelin Volkan (2020) states that the connection between sexual behaviors in fruit flies and humans is not exactly comparable, as human sexual behaviors are regulated by a more complex network of genes, hormones, and neural circuits. Nevertheless, the fundamental mechanisms driving experience-dependent effects on behavior via changes in gene expression and neural circuit function are likely to be conserved across many animal species from insects to humans.

CHAPTER 3

Built-in transference

Before starting Judy's analysis Dr. Rowan had seen her face to face once a week for two years. Now Judy would come to the office four times a week and lie on his psychoanalytic couch, with him sitting behind her. Dr. Rowan was going to be another type of therapist and, psychologically speaking, another person for Judy. Because of this, I discussed a concept I called *"built-in transference"* (Volkan, 2010a) with Dr. Rowan before Judy's analysis started.

Let us consider an analysand who has a history of one or more previous treatments in which experiences with and feelings toward the analyst or therapist had developed and were or were not explored in depth. As this patient enters a new treatment, it is likely that he or she will carry a *built-in transference*. That is, this person may unconsciously relate to the present analyst as an extension of, and thus not clearly separate from, the past analyst or therapist, even if the capacity to distinguish between them intellectually is intact. The analyst, who was not present during the patient's previous treatment, naturally has no knowledge about the experiences, expectations, and feelings unexplored there, factors that may carry over into their work together. In turn, the patient, although unaware of it, is anticipating certain responses from the new analyst, and yet is puzzled when the new analyst does not behave in a particular way.

Twenty-four-year-old Alex started his analysis four times a week while attending a university away from home. He was in analysis for three years before his graduation and return to his home city. His analyst told him to continue his treatment, so Alex found a new analyst. I was this analyst's supervisor. Soon after beginning his new analysis, this young man brought an apple to his new analyst and wanted him to accept it as a gift. The new analyst's first thoughts were, "My patient is giving me an apple like a little boy who wishes to please a teacher." My supervisee was puzzled, and he did not accept Alex's gift but asked his analysand to be curious about why he offered it. Alex felt very disappointed and angry. My supervisee, and later I, learned the following: Alex's previous analyst had been concerned about his patient's ability to control his impulse to spend money sent to him monthly by his parents. Thus, this previous analyst had asked Alex to establish a joint bank account with him, and his patient agreed. Accordingly, this young man could not withdraw funds from his bank without his previous analyst's permission and signature.

My supervisee and I had never heard of an analyst having a joint bank account with the person in analysis on the couch. This arrangement, as well as other similar ones with the previous analyst, apparently lasted for three years until Alex returned home. My supervisee and I concluded that Alex, with his built-in transference, had externalized the image of his previous analyst onto my supervisee and behaved as if his new analyst was an external superego like his previous one. Accordingly, Alex brought an apple to the new analyst in order to please and bribe an externalized superego.

We can easily imagine that Alex's bringing an apple to his new analyst soon after starting his analysis had other meanings, mostly stemming from the patient's early childhood conflicts. The new analyst and I, however, thought that if the built-in transference was not dealt with, it would make it difficult to understand and address such childhood conflicts. The analyst needed to separate his own analytic image from the external superego image of the former analyst, and also directly and indirectly inform his analysand as to how they would work together and develop a therapeutic alliance. My supervisee told Alex the following: "When we became curious about your bringing me an apple, we learned how you and your previous analyst worked together. In this room we will remain curious about your actions instead of my interfering with them by making arrangements with you. This is why I did not accept the apple as a gift. When I did not accept the apple as your gift you were angry and you shouted. But the ceiling did not fall on us. You and I tolerated seeing your rage. The crucial thing is your feeling free to tell me what comes to your mind about what happened between us and express your emotions. I thought that when you wanted to give me a gift it was because you might wish me to give you something in return. Let your mind wander and see if we can find meanings about what had happened between us."

Often, we hear of scenarios in which an analyst puts a patient on the couch for the first time after having worked with this patient face to face for months and even years. This also brings about a built-in transference situation. This situation can be workable, but the analyst needs to pay the necessary attention to it. When a patient's "therapist" becomes an "analyst," the patient most likely and mostly unconsciously, will perceive that the person who has been treating him or her has changed or has been "lost." The patient will bring the unfinished transference expectations of the "therapist" to the "new analyst." The patient may even need time to mourn the "loss" of the therapist.

I wanted to explore with Dr. Rowan the dominant aspect of Judy's transference expectations of him when he functioned as a therapist. Dr. Rowan had felt that therapy was not successful because Judy had not developed a "workable transference." But Judy stayed in therapy for two years and never wished to end it. Obviously, she used her therapist's image to respond to some unconscious expectations, but at this time Dr. Rowan could not describe them.

When Dr. Rowan was presenting Judy's background history to me, I noticed that while Judy was meeting with her therapist once a week, she was also calling her brother almost daily and telling her brother the details of her "hunting" activities. I noted too that Dr. Rowan had not been curious about why Judy was doing this. When I heard about Judy's special relationship with her bother that had started in childhood, the concept of "twinning" came to my mind.

CHAPTER 4

Twinning

Gabriele Ast and I described twinning in our book on the psychology of sibling relationships (Volkan & Ast, 1997). Using this term, we referred to certain activities, as well as ego functions, shared by two, even sometimes more than two, children who usually are siblings, even twins, and sometimes not siblings, in order to make an adjustment to their external and internal lives (see also Ainslie, 1997; Greenacre, 1952). With twinning, children replace their difficulties that stem from a lack of necessary maternal care in the external world and bad parental experiences. Internally, through twinning a child finds a way to deal with separation–individuation issues as described by Margaret Mahler (1968). The twinning reflects a lack of autonomy.

Let us compare twinning with imaginary companions. Sigmund Freud (1919a) described how an uncanny effect takes place when the distinction between imagination and reality is effaced. As an example of common uncanny themes, he referred to the reality of death and a mourner's reanimation of the dead. When the uncanny comes from infantile complexes, psychical reality may take place of material reality in the child's mind. For example, Donald Winnicott (1945), Wilfred Bion (1950), Selma Fraiberg (1959), Humberto Nágera (1969), and

Sheldon Bach (1977) wrote about imaginary companions and imaginary twins. They examined how the development of such imaginary images are defenses for childhood anxieties against integration of object and self-images and psychic devices against splitting of such images and narcissistic disturbances.

Gabriele Ast and I (Volkan & Ast, 1997) wrote that when a child creates an imaginary companion to respond to her loneliness, this companion is a fantasized and wished-for object image. We added that there is a major difference between an imaginary companion and a living real person whom the child imagines as her "twin." The *reality* of the interactions between twinning children makes internalization of their experiences a concrete factor, which influences the structures of their internal worlds more than would the experiences with an imaginary companion. The imaginary companion is under the absolute control of its creator, while a "twin," as a real person, cannot be fully controlled— a negotiation with the other is required, making the twinning experience more complex.

In the psychoanalytic literature there is extensive dealing with the psychology of biological twins. It is beyond the scope of this book to review these papers, but in brief they deal with issues such as strong ties or intense sibling rivalry, fantasy of being only half a person, the protracted identification of one twin with the other. Twinning that I describe here is a pathological development as a response to not having an adequate mother and/or having oedipal level traumas that prevent the child from moving up on his or her developmental ladder. I analyzed two persons who were biological twins, one an identical twin and one a nonidentical one. Pathological twinning did not exist in either of them.

Before returning to Judy's case and examining the impact of her twinning experiences with her brother while she was Dr. Rowan's psychotherapy patient, I will give two examples of twinning. The first one describes a youngster's observable behavior patterns that illustrate twinning, and the second example focuses on the role of twinning in responding to unconscious psychological wishes.

Steven Nickman's (1985) description of fourteen-year-old Bill's "blood brotherhood" is, I believe, a good example of observable activities that suggests the existence of twinning in children. Bill formed a "pact" with a friend, not a sibling. The two youngsters rubbed each other's knuckles with sandpaper until they bled. Then they mixed their blood. Nickman writes that these two children "were convinced that they were biological siblings because they were both adopted and had a similar interest" (p. 375).

The second case, fifty-two-year-old Herman, sought treatment because, like Judy, he had a hunger for good maternal care in childhood, and as an adult he could not give up an unusual compulsive sexual activity. I was the supervisor of his German psychoanalyst. Herman, in Germany, was married for the first time at the age of forty-three and lived in an apartment. Two years after his marriage, he put a bed and a computer in a windowless dark space in the apartment and began spending many hours there each day, even sleeping there at night. He compulsively masturbated in this place. Accompanying his masturbatory activities, he would cut out pornographic pictures of naked women from magazines. Sometimes he would collage torn-apart pictures and frame them. When his dark space became filled with these pictures, his wife urged him to seek psychoanalysis.

Elsewhere I published the story of Herman's psychoanalytic process from its beginning to its termination (Volkan, 2010a). Here I will focus only on why Herman had a twinning experience in childhood with a girl in his neighborhood, how he repeated this in adulthood with his wife, and how his need to find a good mother was the main cause of his compulsive masturbation. In many ways, Herman's story will help us to understand Judy's internal world and her compulsive sexual activities.

Herman's mother was the second wife of Herman's father. Six weeks after Herman was born his mother developed pneumonia and died. For the next few months neighbors took care of baby Herman and his father searched for a third wife in order to find someone to look after the baby right away. This was in post-World War II Germany, and the woman he found, Mathilde, was a German refugee from the Soviet-occupied East. While escaping to Germany to avoid the advancing Soviets, she had been raped by Russian soldiers and later aborted twin fetuses. She was a traumatized person looking for a home. She agreed to marry Herman's father without love between them, and without knowing much about him.

Due to his job requirements, Herman's father was not around much and Mathilde took care of his baby. As a child, Herman was never told that Mathilde was not his biological mother, although he slept in a room where his biological mother's picture hung on the wall. Mathilde did not provide the necessary psychological support for her stepson. Herman recalled having temper tantrums and screaming spells as a child. Sometimes Mathilde would dress him as a girl.

Herman's most important memory concerns Mathilde taking him three times every week throughout his childhood to two cemeteries where they placed or planted flowers on the graves of her husband's two former wives. When Herman recalled this, he thought that Mathilde's invitation to the two graves was casual, like asking someone to go to a coffee shop—a routine event in Herman's childhood.

Most likely, Mathilde had this unusual habit due to her own patho-logical mourning over losing her two fetuses. Not unlike Otto Fenichel's patient I described above, little Herman was preoccupied with graves. Only during his analysis would Herman become aware of how these visits to the graves had induced an unconscious fantasy in his mind that dead persons may come back to life. This fantasy was linked to a wish to find a good mother as well as fear of her.

At age five Herman met a girl in the neighborhood who was a year or two older than he. They formed twinning between themselves. This included compulsive mutual masturbation activities, almost daily. When he was eleven years old the girl found a boyfriend and left Herman.

Here I will not describe in detail Herman's life, except to report that as an adult he was a male nurse taking care of old women who were in their last days of life. His work helped them remain alive longer, but there were times when he would interfere with their physical care, which would induce early death.

When Herman was forty-three years old he met Grete. He learned that as a child Grete was repeatedly sexually abused by her father. He perceived her to be a "dead person," as he thought her father had "killed" her soul. Grete's father was a hunter who brought home his kill, so as a child she was often exposed to dead animals and had seen pools of blood in their house. Herman's father, like Grete's, had also routinely brought home dead animals when his son was a little boy. Grete was interested in ancient Egyptian death rituals, as was Herman. His learning about Grete's background was the main factor in his quick decision to marry her. Until then Herman had been a bachelor.

After they were married, Herman and Grete developed a ritual accompanying sex. First they would take showers and clean themselves, and while doing so, Herman was conscious of the fact that urine and feces are removed from dead bodies before they are buried and sent to another world. Herman and Grete made love while they listened to specific music in a room with burning candles. These activities gave him the deepest joy, a religious-like experience in which he was conscious of his notion to bring Grete "back to life" through sex.

Only during his analysis did Herman become aware that with Grete he was repeating his twinning with his childhood neighbor. His wish was to bring to life his fantasied "dead mother" image by experiencing sexual pleasure with someone who would respond to his hunger for maternal love, love that he could not receive from Mathilde. In analysis he also recalled imagining, as a child, his father's two dead wives coming out of their graves during his cemetery visits with Mathilde, and being frightened of this possibility.

About two years after their marriage, Grete seemed to become tired of their sexual rituals and went into psychoanalytic psychotherapy. By saying that she was suffering from cystitis, she began refusing to join Herman in these rituals. Whenever his wish to crawl into her bed, grab her breasts, or penetrate her was rejected, Herman felt like a "wounded animal." His analyst and I learned that Herman had begun his addiction to ritualistic masturbation after having these feelings. The dark windowless place itself represented a tomb for Herman where the mother figures were put in frames. Many times a leg or arm would protrude from a frame, suggesting a woman was trying to get out of an enclosed space (a grave).

Herman's psychoanalysis, which took a little over seven years, was a successful one. He gave up his addiction to masturbation. He and his wife became close and began to have only "normal" sexual activities. While supervising his analysis, I learned a great deal about twinning as an expression of a patient's wish to find a mother image that would fulfill the need for good mother care through arousal of sexual feelings.

As I listened to Dr. Rowan, I agreed with him and noted that Judy too was searching for an imagined good object to respond to her hunger for good maternal care. But I also sensed that her twinning transference to her brother might be a big factor in her not developing a *workable transference* with her psychotherapist. She was forcing, unconsciously, her therapist to function like an "external superego" without having a positive impact on her pathological behavior pattern. Judy was using Dr. Rowan as her "despotic father" and then defeating him. While also perceiving him as a mother figure that could be bought with Judy's payments for her therapy sessions, he could be kept emotionally away. Dr. Rowan had a habit of getting paid after each session, his patients leaving money on the desk in his office as they left. Judy did the same, but many times, by "accident," she would leave more money than was required for a single session. I noted that during her psychotherapy the reasons for these "accidents" were never discussed. Meanwhile, Judy was continuing her twinning with her brother. I noted that when Judy became an analysand on Dr. Rowan's couch, her analyst would need to recognize and deal with Judy's twinning activities in order to create a workable therapeutic environment.

CHAPTER 5

Judy's analysis begins: Establishing a psychoanalytic foundation and linking interpretations

After lying on Dr. Rowan's psychoanalytic couch, the first thing Judy spoke about was her noticing Dr. Rowan's medical school diploma on the wall, as if for the first time. She asked: "Are you a specialist in treating sexual problems?" Dr. Rowan sensed that his patient was referring to the big change in the therapeutic mode, her lying on a couch instead of sitting on a chair, and wondering who her "new" analyst was. Dr. Rowan stayed silent. Then the patient started to talk about a loss in her childhood—moving to a different location and leaving a friend behind. She was not consciously linking what she was saying to her losing her "therapist." She recalled how at this new place her father beat her badly and her mother did not interfere. Then she reported a fantasy of being in a car accident while not wearing her safety belt. Then Judy told Dr. Rowan that the day before coming to her first psychoanalytic session she went shopping, bought a chair and took it to her home. She stated that the chair, she bought was the same type of chair that she previously sat on in Dr. Rowan's office.

The analyst realized that after losing Dr. Rowan as a therapist, Judy was wondering who he was as an analyst and linking her present loss with a loss in her childhood. Would her "new" analyst be like her father and punish her? Can she remove her safety belt? Dr. Rowan also became aware that Judy, in order to deal with her loss, had bought a chair that symbolized her previous therapeutic togetherness with Dr. Rowan. Keeping in mind the concept of built-in transference, Dr. Rowan spoke: "We are facing a big change in our meeting style. We have been working face to face for two years. Now I have begun sitting behind you. I am the same person; my therapeutic approach will be different. Continue telling me whatever comes to your mind. I will listen and I will speak when I believe that it will be useful for us."

Starting with her first session on the couch, Judy referred to her experiences with her brother. We realized why Judy had sought treatment two years before. As his wedding day approached, Judy's brother had begun withdrawing from twinning with Judy. Her sensing this was a reason she searched for help from another source. However, she was still calling and sharing her hunting activities with her brother; except now her brother would reply only with a few sentences. Later, her brother became more interested in his son than in talking with his sister about her hunting experiences. He wanted Judy to develop a relationship with the boy and suggested she come to his house once a week at a scheduled time and stay alone with his son for a short while. Judy did not want to have weekly "appointments" with the little boy. She also did not feel close to her brother's wife.

My initial talks with Dr. Rowan involved how to initiate communication with Judy after she started using his couch and how to create a psychoanalytic foundation for their future work together. I suggested that his initial communications should aim to prepare Judy to be curious about her internal psychological processes; in other words, to help her develop an analytic mindset.

My advice to Dr. Rowan was to make sounds such as as, "Hmm," or remarks such as, "Go on. Let's see what else will come to your mind," so Judy would not feel lonely after the loss of their previous relationship, which included continuous dialogues, questions, and answers. I also advised Dr. Rowan to be curious about psychological links between topics Judy mentioned, such as finding a connection between the patient losing her "therapist" and how she had moved to a new location during her childhood and lost a friend. I wanted to help Dr. Rowan to make "*linking interpretations*" only at this stage and not to go any deeper.

Interpretation refers to the analyst making repressed content available to the patient. For decades, interpretation was considered the crucial therapeutic tool, but today we know that it makes up only a portion of the necessary processes involved in the analysand-analyst relationship that lead to internal structural changes in a patient. Furthermore, as time went on, this term became one of the most blurred of psychoanalytic concepts (Tähkä, 1993). Today, while attending some professional meetings, I hear some clinicians use the word "interpretation" for almost all communications from analysts, and this saddens me.

There are different types of interpretations. I (Volkan, 2010a) suggest the analyst should make linking interpretations at the beginning of an analysis, even before making "preparatory interpretations" (Loewenstein, 1951, 1958). The time for making deep genetic and transference interpretations will come later. Peter Giovacchini (1969, 1972) was the first analyst who described linking interpretations, and I expanded them further (Volkan, 1976, 1987, 2010a). Giovacchini based his description of linking interpretation on Freud's (1900a) concept of *day residue* in dreams. As day residue, insignificant impressions derived from the real world—seeing a police cruiser chasing a speeding car on the highway or passing a billboard depicting a smiling woman holding a milk bottle—join infantile aggressive or sexual wishes to initiate the content of dreams. Giovacchini applied Freud's understanding of day residue to the clinical setting, stating, "An interpretation may make a causal connection by referring to the day residue which may be the stimulus for the flow of the patient's associations or for some otherwise unexplainable behavior" (1969, p. 180). For example, while on the couch, a female patient looked at the ceiling and said that blood was dripping from holes in the ceiling tiles. I connected this bizarre perception with the patient's earlier statement that she had just begun menstruating, thus linking her identification of her bleeding body with a "bleeding" environment.

One analysand at the beginning phase of his analysis began a session by reporting that on his way to his analyst's office he thought that one of the tires of his car was becoming flat. He talked about stopping his car to check the tires before arriving at the parking lot and checking the tires once more after parking it. Toward the end of the session, lowering his voice, he told his analyst that the day before he had taken an important examination that had four parts. He was sure that he had done well in answering the first three parts, but he was doubtful if he would get a passing grade for the fourth part. He seemed embarrassed. The analyst linked his four-part examination with the four tires of his car of which the one imagined bad tire corresponded to his patient's worry about failing one part of the examination. Linking interpretations make analysands more psychologically minded and ready to observe their psychic processes without undue anxiety or resistance. The analysand is then increasingly prepared to produce material that is more sensitive.

Elsewhere, after telling the story of the analysand who was preoccupied with his car's tires, I wrote about what an analyst communicates to a new analysand by making linking interpretations:

1. I am with you. I am listening to you carefully and finding links between the two (or more) stories you reported.

2. I am showing you what we will be interested in during our time together. I am *not* deeply interested in all the external events you presented to me. Instead, from within what is presented, we will choose an external event (e.g. doing poorly on ¼ of an examination) that resonates in your internal world and then later becomes "alive" again in yet another external event (e.g. imagining that one of four tires is bad). There is an intertwining of external and internal events. We will be curious about what kinds of internal, unconscious phenomena are reflected and re-enacted in external events.

3. We will pay attention to symbols (e.g., the tires) and wonder about their purpose.

4. There are deeper meanings to the things you report while lying on the couch.

5. I am teaching you to bring your external world and its symbolic representations to sessions and, in doing so, to me. (There is meaning in your reliving the examination situation on your way in to see me.) You will experience things in relation to me, something that is technically called *transference manifestation*. (Volkan, 2010a, pp. 34–35)

The concept of linking interpretation is akin to Rudolph Loewenstein's (1951, 1958) description of *preparatory interpretations*. Linking interpretations illustrate the influence of an external event on the patient's internal world and inspire the patient's curiosity about the interaction between external events and internal processes. In contrast, Loewenstein's preparatory interpretations primarily focus on how something in a patient's internal world stimulates expected and similar behavior in certain circumstances.

Let us consider a young man who, at the initial phase of his analysis, gives several examples illustrating how he consistently tries to avoid competition. Telling him that he is bound in some kind of unconscious rivalry as demonstrated in his avoidance of competition is an example of preparatory interpretation. By connecting the patient's behavior and internal motives, the analyst awakens the patient's curiosity about what might motivate such patterns and internal phenomena. Linking interpretations demonstrate the effect of the external on the internal, whereas preparatory interpretations reflect the internal's effect on the external. Like linking interpretations, preparatory interpretations are also a means of developing the therapeutic alliance.

CHAPTER 6

The first dream and Judy's first year of analysis

During the middle of the second month of her analysis Judy had to go to Africa as part of her job and be away from Dr. Rowan for three weeks. She could not cancel the trip. This obviously complicated starting an analytic process. Just before leaving, Judy filled her sessions by reporting that she had begun eating constantly "like a crazy person" while worrying that she might eat something that would be harmful. She reported visual fantasies of babies staring at apples.

Using the concept of linking interpretation, Dr. Rowan verbalized the strong possibility that there was a connection between Judy's upcoming separation from her analyst and its associated feeling of loss with her search for good and harmless nutrition. Dr. Rowan also linked Judy's reaction to this separation with many separations she had experienced as a child. In order to inform Judy about the importance of symbols, he added that the apples in her visual fantasies might be symbols of maternal breasts.

Judy's absence from her analysis for three weeks led to Dr. Rowan and Judy coming up with an agreement related to a *real-world issue*. Dr. Rowan agreed not to charge Judy for missing hours during her future trips as long as he knew about them two months ahead of time and if he could arrange to see other patients during these available hours. Judy already had arranged with her business firm not to schedule as much travel for her as they had in the past. The trip to Africa had already been planned as had another one-week trip to France, which took place soon after Judy came back from Africa. Before going to France, Judy visited a dietitian to find out what was best for her to eat. On Dr. Rowan's couch she wanted to fall asleep like a baby.

Apparently, during her face-to-face work with Dr. Rowan, Judy very rarely mentioned her dreams. Now she reported a dream. In it she was on a ship in the sea on a stormy night. Suddenly she turned into a pirate. Discussing the manifest content of this dream, Dr. Rowan and I connected it to her separations from her analyst by traveling to Africa and France. At another level she might also be responding to losing her "therapist Dr. Rowan"; she was lost in the stormy sea. In her mind, she was linking her current losses with her physical and psychological childhood losses: needed maternal care and frequent moves from one location to another.

Her turning into a pirate might be an effort that illustrates *reaching up*. The concept, "reaching up," first described by Bryce Boyer (1983, 1999), refers to an individual's way of escaping from an anxiety-provoking conflict belonging to a lower-level childhood development. For example, a patient's constant and sometimes dramatic preoccupation with oedipal issues can be in the service of covering up a more hurtful preoedipal issue. Judy turning into a pirate represented her wish to reach up to her father as a way to escape her hunger for maternal care. As I stated earlier, during her psychotherapy Judy had connected her choice of profession with her father's profession. Her recent trips to Africa and France were like her father's frequent activities during her childhood. As a child, when she "reached up," she found a despotic father, a pirate. In her early teen years, her father would be angry if she showed an interest in boys. She had faced molestation as well. Being a pirate also represented her childhood rage against both her mother and father. As a child she could not name her feelings.

Her *first dream* was a kind of "summary" of what Dr. Rowan would deal with in her analysis, what he would analyze. Dr. Rowan did not share what we thought about Judy's first dream in her analysis with his patient. Although she might agree with what had come to our minds, an intellectual discussion of genetic factors of her psyche at this phase of their work would not be helpful.

During the first year of her analysis, Judy kept making direct or symbolic references to her childhood "hunger" for maternal care and primarily sought answers *through actions* in addition to her hunting behavior, such as trying out different kinds of food. She would have many short dreams and fantasies about eating this or that, and had visions of babies looking at apples. She started visiting several dieticians but was disappointed in them. I must add here that Judy's weight remained the same during her work with Dr. Rowan.

Judy brought short dreams to her sessions. In most of them she saw herself in water, in a lake with a big tree sticking out of it. I thought that her being in the lake was a symbolic expression of her difficulties in separation–individuation from her mother and that the tree stood for a phallus, the oedipal father. She wanted to get to this tree, and sometimes she tried to climb it without knowing where she would go next. At this time I thought that the theme of these dreams reflected her wish to "reach up." Later, in Chapter 13, I will return to Judy's lake dreams.

In the manifest content of her dreams, Dr. Rowan and I could also observe her constant references to her childhood rage. For example, she had a dream in which she was traveling with her mother in an airplane. When the plane landed at a new airport and her mother was getting out of the plane, suddenly her mother's head separated from her body and fell to the ground. In the dream, Judy did not know who or what had cut off her mother's head. In addition to these dreams, she once had an argument with a woman who had come to her apartment to fix her curtains. Judy sensed that she had a "devil" in her.

During the first year of her analysis, she also experienced a brand-new bodily symptom. She involuntarily experienced teeth grinding. In this symptom we noted her wish for food and her rage that started her grinding her teeth (oral anger) and in turn hurting herself. This would continue for many months.

Judy talked about her jealousy whenever she saw parents with their children and these parents' love for their children. Following such an observation she had a dream. She was in a tunnel where there was a monster (her childhood rage, her despotic father, her molester). When she got out of the tunnel, she found a "lover." This briefly made her happy.

But she could not even remember this lover's name. Who was he? Would he really love her, or would he beat or molest her? She became sad.

Judy began giving detailed information about her childhood. For example, she would describe how no one caressed her lovingly when she was a child. She would give the details of her father beating her and her brother. Referring to her hunting behavior she would repeat how she knew she was searching for someone to cuddle her. She wanted to find out if providing "good food" for someone or something was possible. She bought a pot of flowers and wanted to be sure that she could keep the plant healthy by watering it regularly. This "hobby" however was short lived. She did not buy another pot of flowers, but she continued hunting men.

One day, as soon as she entered Dr. Rowan's office, she smelled food, as if Dr. Rowan's office was a kitchen. I told Dr. Rowan to focus on this and tell Judy how she had brought her "hungry self" to his office between the two of them and how this was an important development in their work of observing and examining together her thoughts and feelings. I wanted Dr. Rowan to help Judy develop her transference expectations. When he suggested to Judy that she stay with her smelling food in his office, nothing new developed.

There were other occasions when we could recognize transference issues. Earlier I had mentioned that Judy bought a chair identical to the chair she was sitting on when she was seeing Dr. Rowan face to face. Now she reported buying a robe. She had chosen this garment, used for cuddling, because its color was the same as that of the lampshades in her analyst's office. But, once more, she could not continue to talk about Dr. Rowan and bring out her transference expectations fully to the analytic work.

I sensed that Dr. Rowan himself was hesitant to allow Judy's transference to develop and be a focus of Judy's analysis. Was he resisting becoming another "lover" in Judy's mind? As a supervisor, I am very careful not to act as an analyst who investigates his or her supervisee's internal world; as a supervisor I do not become a therapist for my supervisee.

I found a way to approach Dr. Rowan's hesitancy. I suggested to him that he could refer to Judy's "lovers," as A, B, C instead of repeating their real names. In reality these "lovers" had their own names and personality organizations, but there was no need for us to know each lover's name. They all functioned as the same symbol for Judy—as a constantly searched-for object that would provide cuddling, maternal care, and not be a despotic father or a "molester"—for however short a time. Referring to the first letter of his first name, I told Dr. Rowan that sometime during her analysis Judy most likely would be preoccupied with "R." Then I reminded him that R would *not behave* like A, B, C. I added that he is someone with a psychoanalytic identity who protects a therapeutic atmosphere and continues to be curious. I asked him directly, "Would you ever imagine going to bed with Judy?" Dr. Rowan loudly said, "No." Then, I spoke: "See, we have no problem."

Soon I noticed that while talking to his patient Dr. Rowan began referring to the men his patient was hunting as A, B, C. I was pleased to note that at the same time, without my suggestion, he used a symbolic word, this time describing his analysand. He told Judy that she was a "honey bee," going from one flower to another, but not finding the food she was looking for. He wondered out loud if the honey bee was getting tired of this unending search. Soon we noticed that Judy was slowing down her hunting activities. Instead, she started to call some previous "lovers" with whom she had stayed longer than one night and wanted to know what they were doing. Sometimes she would meet with them. In one session she said: "I look in the mirror and see myself as a beautiful woman. But I can't give up my hunting relationships. Every night I need to hold someone and sleep. If I learn to value myself, perhaps I will stop this habit."

As months passed Judy declared that it would be better to call herself an "ant" instead of a "honey bee." "Ants face obstacles," she said, "and they turn around and around." She was tired of being an ant, but could not yet give up her sexual addiction. When Judy called herself an ant, I realized that I had sometimes thought of her as an ant when Dr. Rowan would tell me how, during her sessions, very often she would go from one topic to another, from talking about a man she had hunted to going to see a movie, to an event at work, to reading a book, to reporting the weather, and so on. I imagined that when her mother punished her during her childhood by denying her food and making her experience hunger, she might have had a fantasy of finding something to eat if she turned around and around like an ant. If she did have such a fantasy, it was an unconscious one.

By the end of the first year of her analysis, she declared that she had become a "turtle." In fact, the symbol she used for herself at this time was a fitting one. The turtle represented her slowing down her hunting activities and keeping her hunger under cover.

After her brother became more and more interested in his son and his wife and spent less time with his sister on the phone, Judy's main transference relationship was with a dog. A primary reason for Judy's not developing a workable transference during the first year of her analysis was her intense relationship with this dog. Meanwhile I had no idea and expectation that Judy would later use the symbols of A, B, C for coming closer to R, Dr. Rowan. We will return to this topic after I describe animals on the couch in the next chapter and Judy's relationship with her dog in Chapter 8.

CHAPTER 7

Animals, birds, fish, or insects "on the couch"

Our analysands, children or adults, often mention different kinds animals, birds, fish or insects during their treatment sessions and see them in their dreams. In *The Interpretation of Dreams* Sigmund Freud (1900a) wrote that a snake can stand for a phallus. Two of his famous cases are known as "Rat Man," a lawyer nearly thirty years of age who had an obsession with rats (Freud, 1909d), and "Wolf Man" who was in his early twenties when he first came to see Freud and who had wolf phobia as well as a fear of lions and other animals (Freud, 1918b). Another of Freud's famous cases, "Little Hans," a five-year-old child, had a phobia of horses (Freud, 1909b).

After Freud, throughout many years, psychoanalysts wrote about the symbolic meanings of animals, birds, fish, or insects and what they meant for some patients (e.g. Burlingham, 1952; Kupfermann, 1977; Sanford, 1966; Searles, 1960; Sherick, 1981; Sperling, 1952; Volkan & Ast, 1994, 1997). But, generally speaking, in the psychoanalytic literature, examining animals and other nonhuman creatures "on the couch" was rare. To fill this vacuum, Salman Akhtar and I edited two volumes and published our colleagues' and our psychoanalytic findings on different animals, birds, fish, and insects utilized as different symbols and images for individuals as well as in large-group cultures (Akhtar & Volkan, 2005a, 2005b).

I will tell two stories explaining why I have always been interested in paying attention to cats "on my couch." I was born to Turkish parents on the Mediterranean island Cyprus, the place of my first memory: losing my beloved cat Rengin when I was five years old. I do not recall if Rengin was a female or male cat. In Turkish its name refers to its being colorful. As an adult, when I visualize it, I see a mixture of colors I believe representing my different childhood feelings. Rengin was my pet when my father was an elementary school master in a village in Cyprus. When the three-month-long summer vacations came, the family would set out by bus for Nicosia, the capital city of Cyprus, where we had our family house. In my memory, I am on the bus holding Rengin on my lap. When the bus stopped to pick up other travelers, my cat leapt out and disappeared. Later I was told that a search had ensued but Rengin could not be found. I experienced deep emotions, the primary one was grief, which I could name only after I grew up. In my biography, written by Ferhat Atik (2019), I describe how losing Rengin would come to my mind whenever I faced a significant loss in my life.

I came to the United States in 1957 about six months after graduating from Ankara University's Medical School in Turkey. A year after my arrival in the United States, I began my training in psychiatry at the Memorial Hospital of the University of North Carolina in Chapel Hill. In those days, the main emphasis of psychiatric education in the United States was how to evaluate and treat patients via a psychodynamic approach. Also in those days, patients could stay at a university hospital for a long time, many months and even sometimes over a year. During the third year of my training I was assigned to take care of a mentally very troubled hospitalized woman, Samantha. Looking back, I can say that through observing her and learning, Samantha became my first teacher about early object relations. I published Samantha's story in one of my first books (Volkan, 1976). Here I will describe her using her two cats as externalized versions of her internal self-images. This will be useful in understanding how Judy's dog was primarily an externalized version of her internal self- and object images.

Samantha was a thirty-one-year-old married woman. I saw her for nine months, almost daily, while she was hospitalized. After she left the hospital, for the next two years she would come to see me infrequently. She was still not well. Then I left North Carolina and moved to Virginia and had no more contact with her.

While she was an inpatient, Samantha was able to describe, in her own way, the details of a fragmentation of her personality. She had a "left side" and a "right side" with a division between the two. She called this division (splitting her libidinally and aggressively invested self- and internalized object images) a "bar" and stated that there was no place to land on it. She had many "selves" on both the left and right sides that came and went, none remaining for any length of time. She also reported that at times she would lose this "double personality" and regress to what she named a "complete backwards" state.

I became aware of how she behaved while she was on her left or right sides or the state of "complete backwards." When she was controlled by her "left side" she spoke softly, and talked with me seductively and gently. When the "right side" dominated, she spoke roughly and exhibited a temper to the point of throwing things at me. When in her "complete backwards" state, she lay speechless and motionless in the fetal position, eyelids heavy, oblivious of others. Slowly I would learn her life story and why she had to be hospitalized.

Samantha was the firstborn in a family in which the father was only marginally involved; he was passive and rather colorless. Emotionally unprepared for motherhood, her mother raised her daughter according to the advice of a book that recommended leaving babies alone and refraining from unnecessary handling and affectionate play. As a young woman Samantha's mother was not prepared to be a housewife, and had a fantasy of becoming a concert pianist. In a sense she was "forced" to marry her rich and much older husband in the small town where they lived. Soon she became pregnant with Samantha. To Samantha's mother, the child was a doll who would, in the course of time, gratify her mother by becoming a famous musician. As baby Samantha lay in her crib or played in her playpen without tactile stimulation or other bodily contact, her mother played the piano endlessly. The mother's practical competence was so lacking that Samantha developed long crying spells at the age of only a few months. The physician who had to be called declared the infant "hungry" and advised bottle-feeding. We can imagine her main hunger, like Judy's, was for maternal care and love.

Samantha's mother had "musical communication" with her daughter and tried to teach the child to play the piano at an early age. Samantha's limited musical accomplishment disappointed her mother's hopes, however, and when another girl was born, thirteen years after Samantha, the mother transferred her musical interests and ambitions to the younger child. When Samantha was seventeen years old, her parents urged her to marry a man. She repeated her mother's history by marrying a man she did not know. She had difficulty handling the ordinary responsibilities of being a wife, and often retreated under stress to her mother's home, near which she and her husband resided.

Seven years before she was hospitalized at the Memorial Hospital in Chapel Hill, North Carolina, Samantha had moved to Austria with her husband and young daughter because of her husband's business. In her mind, now she was in "the most musical country of the world"; even her neighbors, as it happened, were musically inclined and often played the piano. The "musical environment" in this distant land represented her own early "musical environment" at home with her mother; it was in Austria that she regressed, sometimes exhibiting a psychotic state.

The family had taken their cats—Maxie, a male, and Marie Jane, a female—to Europe with them. Samantha anthropomorphically endowed Marie Jane with gentleness and Maxie with strength and power, representing her own two "sides." When I learned this, I realized that, at the hospital when she was on her "left" or "right" sides she was exhibiting cat-like behavior. When she felt gentle, she worked her hands like the paws of a kitten kneading its mother's belly while nursing; aggression, on the other hand, she expressed with clawing gestures. She once made a significant slip of the tongue, saying that she had "tasted" her cats when she meant to say she had "chased" them, revealing how her cats stood for her internalized split images.

As her treatment progressed, it came out that Marie Jane had met her end after falling from a window and going into convulsions. (It was unclear whether Samantha had actually pushed her, though she blamed the maid for the accident.) When it happened, Samantha reported, she had not wept, but assumed the stillness and composure she had attributed to Marie Jane. Now the balance between the "libidinal" cat and the "aggressive" one was disturbed. She became greatly concerned about and fearful of the "wildness" she saw in Maxie after

Marie Jane died. She persuaded her husband to have Maxie euthanized, and afterwards felt "killed inside," as she said, for she had lost her split self- and object-images. It was at this point that she first regressed to the state she designated "the complete backwards." Her husband brought her back to the United States and she was hospitalized.

After moving to Virginia and becoming a faculty member of the Department of Psychiatry at the University of Virginia, I continued to be interested in what cats mean for some patients. In one of these volumes Salman Akhtar and I edited, I presented cases to illustrate how cats are used not only as symbols of internalized self- and object images, but also as transitional objects (Volkan, 2005).

At the present time I am supervising the analysis of a patient who sought treatment at the age of forty-one after hitting and killing a cat by accident. She has a history like Judy's; as a child she was deprived of maternal care and love. She was born in a communist country to parents who belonged to a minority ethnic group there. As a small baby she was separated from her parents and put in a communist kindergarten for two years, only allowed to see her parents once or twice a week. She grew up with extreme hunger for maternal care. As an adult, in another country to which she and her family had escaped, she became a physician. Her main "symptom" reflecting her search for maternal love, was taking care of sick people in an extraordinary, almost bizarre, way. If she heard that a person she considered a friend or even an acquaintance was ill, in spite of her busy life, she would drive for hours to another place or even fly to another country to examine and offer care for the sick person. After killing a cat, she began collecting sick or hungry cats whenever she found them in parks or streets. Cats represented her hungry self and she had to feed them. Then this woman started hoarding twenty to thirty cats in her house and garden.

Kevin Volkan (2021), referring to the findings of the Hoarding of Animals Research Consortium at Tufts University School of Veterinary Medicine in Boston, Massachusetts, reminds us that there are 3,000 estimated cases of animal hoarding in the United States per year. He also tells us that in the psychoanalytic literature (see for example, Brien, O'Connor, & Russell-Carroll, 2018; Camps & Le Bigot, 2019) hoarding behavior is not considered an addiction. It is perceived as an obsessional neurosis and is explained by referring to excessive utilization of anal mechanisms, holding on to feces (Freud, 1908b). Kevin Volkan explores hoarding as a multifaceted disorder with biological, social, and psychological dimensions. With case examples, he illustrates how animal hoarding, from a psychoanalytic viewpoint, represents early object loss during the transitional phase of development. The hoarder attempts to gain mastery of his or her psychological deficit through reanimated object images and repetition-compulsion.

Philip Escoll (2005) tells us that, as man's best friend, dogs have become a significant part of human experience and culture for about 12,000 years. He reminds us how dogs function "as siblings, inviting closeness as well as rivalry" (p. 129). He describes the case of Harry, who experienced severe loneliness in his childhood. During his analysis he spoke of his childhood dog named Hero as the central figure in the family with whom he could communicate. "It was most satisfying and great relief for Harry that he could say everything and anything to Hero, which he could not express to his parents or to others. This included his sexual fantasies, his experimentation with masturbation, and the questions and doubts that he had about himself in these areas" (p. 152).

The classical understanding of transference refers to the displacement of behavior and feelings originally directed toward significant figures of one's childhood. The classical view of transference neurosis refers to the displacement of infantile conflicts—between drives and defenses against them—to the analyst. These classical views are inadequate to describe the state of affairs existing between the patient and the significant other (the analyst) when we are dealing with patients like Samantha and Judy. Years ago, before psychoanalysts became seriously interested in object relations, Anna Freud noted that the psychoanalyst trying to treat an individual with primitive personality organization has much in common with the child analyst; not all the relations transferred by the child in analysis are of the sort in which the analyst becomes cathected with libido or aggression. Many are due to *externalizations*, "to processes in which the analyst is used to represent one or the other part of the patient's personality structure" (A. Freud, 1965, p. 41).

We need to differentiate externalization from projection (Berg, 1977; Novick & Kelly, 1970; Volkan, 1995). Projection is used to defend against a specific drive derivative directed against an object. In treating patients with neurotic personality organization we are very familiar with transference projections exhibited side by side with transference displacements. Externalization is an earlier mechanism, one pertaining to aspects of the self as well as aspects of internalized objects. It is similar to Melanie Klein's (1946) term "projective identification." Klein described projective identification as "a combination of splitting off parts of the self and projecting them on to another person" (p. 108). A patient uses externalization if he or she, as a child, faced the extremely difficult task of integrating the various dissonant components of his or her developing self-images as well as internalized object world.

Samantha's case clearly illustrates her externalization and internalization of libidinally and aggressively cathected self- and object images. After having a deprived child image, Judy developed a higher-level self-image with higher-level ego functions which, as an adult, allowed her to have a responsible job. Her higher-level self-image surrounded her hungry self-image, but she could not mend her low-level and high-level self-representations. The task of her high-level part was to be busy externalizing and internalizing her core hungry self and related realistic and fantasied object images with *actions* without finding a solution. Elsewhere, I (Volkan, 1995) described, with detailed case examples, various fates of such unintegrated early childhood self- and object images.

In the next chapter I will describe how Judy used a pet to deal with her core self- and object images.

CHAPTER 8

Judy's dog

As she started her analysis, Judy bought a female puppy. It took some time for Dr. Rowan to mention this puppy during his supervision hours. One day he told me that Judy was spending most of her free time with her pet. She was no longer traveling frequently, but whenever she returned from her trips, her first concern would be her puppy. She wanted to know that the puppy was properly taken care of during her absence. When Dr. Rowan told me the puppy's name it meant nothing to me, but when I wondered why Judy chose this unusual pet name, Dr. Rowan realized that the name was very similar to Judy's mother's name. Let us give a name for Judy's mother and her dog and call Judy's mother *Muriel* and her dog *Muri*. Slowly, Dr. Rowan and I began to understand what Muri stood for to Judy besides being a pet.

At one level, as the name suggests, Muri represented Muriel, the mother. By loving and taking care of Muri, the analysand was creating a caring mother–daughter relationship, in a reverse way; the daughter was looking after the mother. By holding on to this relationship, Judy was trying to prove for herself that it was possible to find a childhood wherein there would be no unsatisfied hunger for maternal care.

The owner of Muri's father also brought her dog to the same dog park where Judy took Muri. It was important for Judy to watch the father dog playing with his daughter dog. Judy needed to observe how a father can play with his daughter. At the dog park, many people seemed to be aware of Judy's special relationship with Muri. They nicknamed her "Muri's mother," in spite of the fact that Muri's real mother sometimes came to the park with her owner.

Dr. Rowan began focusing on Muri during his supervision hours after his analysand reported another one of her visual fantasies in which babies were looking at apples. This time, in her fantasy, Muri was with the babies, an externalized version of the hungry Judy. Around this time, we began noticing that she was becoming more disappointed with her brother. For example, she would complain about how he and his wife attended gatherings without inviting Judy to join them.

Listening to Dr. Rowan, I slowly sensed that Judy was primarily using her dog to find solutions for her psychological problems. She reported how she was overfeeding Muri even when she knew that her dog was no longer hungry. Then we learned that she was writing letters to her dog. This reminded me of Philip Escoll's (2005) patient Harry's communication with his dog Hero. Judy never brought such letters to her sessions, but described what she was writing. She was telling her dog how grateful she was that Muri was teaching her how to love and be loved.

Interestingly, we also learned that Muri was contaminated with Judy's analyst's image. One day Judy described how, after owning her puppy, she had bought a dog collar and a leash. She wanted to take her puppy outside for a walk and teach her how to stay near her by pulling the leash. Then she told Dr. Rowan why she had chosen a special collar and leash. The color of these items, like the bathrobe she purchased earlier, was identical to that of Dr. Rowan's lampshades.

Many of their sessions contained references to Muri as Judy's main transference figure. Dr. Rowan would try to make linking interpretations and connect his analysand's relationship with her childhood. For example, Dr. Rowan would link Judy's overfeeding her dog with her memory of how she could not give up her pacifier to the point of carrying it with her and putting it in her mouth all the way up to starting elementary school. Most of the time, Judy would feel sleepy whenever her analyst tried to put into words his understanding of what Muri meant to his patient. In a sense, Judy would not hear what her analyst was saying. She was continuing to find "solutions" for her psychopathology with actions.

Once she imagined bringing Muri to Dr. Rowan's office and keeping the dog in the car when she went into her session. Then she imagined someone trying to break into the car. In her mind, Muri began to bark loudly, scaring this person away. She then linked what came to her mind to her molestation experience at age five or six. In her fantasy, her dog was a protector – little Judy who could say no to her molester. Her father had told her to stay away from boys, but since he was despotic, a child-beater, and very scary, he could not be a loving protector.

In the next session Judy spoke of a movie, *The King's Speech*. Earlier I had seen this 2010 historical drama in which Colin Firth plays the future King George VI. When I was a child and teenager in Cyprus, then a British colony, there were many school ceremonies during which my classmates and I, even though we were Cypriot Turks, would shout: "Long live King George VI." I had no idea that he had a speech impairment. Because of my history in Cyprus, I was very interested in this film. In the movie, a speech and language therapist helped the future king overcome his stuttering before he could be a "father figure" for his people during World War II.

I wondered about Judy's "hidden" transference expectations of Dr. Rowan. Did she want Dr. Rowan to become a stronger parent figure before she could openly talk about her transference expectations and begin using a workable transference to work through her childhood conflicts linked to deprivations and rage? Dr. Rowan, I learned, was not a fan of movies; he had no knowledge of *The King's Speech*. His attempts to expand upon what Judy wanted to work on did not go deeper. I noticed that Judy, now a turtle in her hunting activities, began renting DVD movies, from *Peter Pan* to *Indiana Jones*, and watching them at night with Muri. She would come to her sessions and give reports about what she and her dog had watched. Dr. Rowan could not make linking interpretations since he did not know the details of these films' stories, and Judy would not tell him the psychological themes in these movies that might be connected to the issues in her life.

One night, Judy and Muri watched *Beaver*, which had become very popular in 2011, the year it hit the movie theaters, and now could be bought as a DVD. In it a depressed man who was the CEO of a toy company is kicked out by his wife and elder son; he is rejected. He develops a new personality represented by a beaver hand puppet, an image of an animal. He, played by Mel Gibson, wears the puppet constantly and communicates as a beaver. This helps him to recover. I will not give a full summary of this film here, but in the end, this man gets rid of the beaver puppet by cutting his arm off at the elbow. After surgery and equipped with a prosthetic hand, he ends up in a psychiatric hospital. Eventually he returns to normal life. Again I wondered if Judy was hoping to find a "healthier" analyst to represent a parental figure that she had missed in her childhood. Dr. Rowan had never seen this film or known its story.

As she approached the end of the first year of lying on Dr. Rowan's couch as his patient, she had to leave for another rather long trip, this time to go to faraway places such as Hong Kong and Singapore. She made good arrangements for Muri's care. She declared, "I am learning to be a responsible caretaker. I can take good care of Muri."

During the first year of analysis, it was clear that Dr. Rowan's patient was not like most analysands. I observed that she could not yet use genetic or transference explanations or interpretations to initiate psychic change. Her primary way of dealing with her problems was through *actions*, which would allow her to externalize and internalize her early realistic and fantasied internal self- and object images. With her sexual addiction she would find only temporary love from a man on whom a love-giving image was externalized. Her interactions with Muri were not like her one-night stands, they were continuous. This allowed her to become a turtle in "hunting" men. The psychological connection of Muri to transference, finding a steady object image in her analyst, remained hidden. The only open connection to Dr. Rowan was the color of the leash that connected him with Muri. When her analyst tried to help her to think more about this, Judy would not express her feelings and thoughts about her analyst. Through her actions related to Muri, she was trying to learn if the existence of continuous motherly care was possible.

I examined in detail the role of analysands' *actions* as resistance, as well as in getting well, in my textbook on psychoanalytic treatment (Volkan, 2010a). Supervising Judy's case taught me more about this subject. In the next two chapters I will review psychoanalytic views on analysands' actions and in Chapter 12 I will describe how she repeated what she was doing with Muri with Albert, a human being.

CHAPTER 9

Analysands' actions

In 1901 Freud wrote about "symptomatic acts," which provide expression of something that the individual does not suspect is in them. He noted that "symptomatic acts" are found in both healthy and neurotic people. Five years later, while telling the story of Dora who was eighteen or nineteen years old when Freud began working with her, Freud described how she "acted out" her essential fantasies and recollections instead of producing them in the treatment (Freud, 1905e, p. 119). In 1907 Freud focused on obsessive actions and compared obsessional individuals' behavior with religious ceremonies, a universal phenomenon. Miserable sinners, he noted, attempt to deal with guilt by participating in religious acts. He regarded obsessional neurosis as a pathological counterpart of involvement in religion. Later he wrote that acting out is not only a resistance; it is also a way of remembering (Freud, 1914g).

Our analysands report their actions that take place outside the office like those Judy repeatedly described, such as her "hunting" activities and relationship with Muri. At other times analysands give a message to the analyst and unconsciously describe a psychological process by action while lying on the couch. For example, a few months after she began lying on my couch, I noticed that Rebecca had something in her mouth and, now and then, she looked as if she were chewing it. I watched during the next several sessions to be sure that she actually did have something in her mouth. I then shared my observation with her.

I learned that Rebecca would put a Life Saver in her mouth just before her sessions started. Life Savers are hard candies invented in Cleveland, Ohio in 1912 that are still popular among many children and adults in the United States. After a few weeks of wondering together about the meaning of the Life Saver, Rebecca began lying on the couch without one. She became flooded with childhood memories of being with her mother who was sitting in their living room stark naked. She would often do this while clinging to Rebecca, holding her tightly on her lap. I slowly learned the meaning of Rebecca's action. Keeping a candy in her mouth was related to her need to find a boundary between herself and the very intrusive mother image she had externalized onto me (Volkan, 2010a). I dealt with Rebecca's flooded emotions by telling her how I noticed them and that she could slow down since we would have time to look at them in a measured fashion. The reader also can guess that the name of the candy, Life Saver, had significant meaning for Rebecca.

Other patients bring a bottle of water or some other object to their analyst's office and put it next to them. Some patients rub the wall next to the couch while talking. All such actions within an analyst's office and their hidden unconscious meanings can be named "*acting in*." The term *acting in* first was used by Meyer Zeligs (1957) when he described patients' postural attitudes and bodily movements as illustrating their unconscious conflicts.

Since psychoanalysis was perceived as a talking cure, the classical psychoanalytic view of action was thought of as something that "impedes the ego from being confronted with unconscious material" (Fenichel, 1945, p. 570). Otto Fenichel argued that an activity "relates only to the present and does not make the patient conscious of being dominated by his past. Analysis should show the past to be effective in the present" (p. 571). In general, *acting out* or *acting in* were considered undesirable in psychoanalysis, a treatment based on verbalization. The concept *acting out* was also applied to habitual impulsivity and socially unacceptable behavior, such as drug addiction and alcoholism (Abt & Weissman, 1965).

Alan Wheelis (1950), while not devaluing the need to work through the analytic process with words, and while stating that an analyst does not persuade the analysand to act in a certain way, wondered to what extent the analysand's activities were involved in resolving intrapsychic problems. During a 1967 panel discussion at the International Psychoanalytical Congress in Copenhagen, Leo Rangell, in a sense, liberated *acting out* from its previously pejorative bias. He pointed out its communicative nature and value in treatment. The paper he gave at this congress on this topic was published a year later (Rangell, 1968). Other well-known analysts joined Leo Rangell. For example, in 1976, Harold Blum described how difficult it is to have a specific definition of *acting out*. He believed that in its classical sense *acting out* is usually a "formidable resistance outside of psycho-analytic scrutiny; but it may also represent efforts to master trauma, and a transference development coincident with analytic work and a step toward sublimated activity" (p. 183).

Samuel Novey (1968) came up with a new term, "*the second look*," an action with therapeutic value. When setting out from Baltimore to spend the weekend in southern Maryland, a man found himself before a small house; he discovered this house to be his birthplace. Hearing this, Novey wrote that the "first and most evident function of revisiting old scenes is the interest of mastering the past. This thesis was developed by Freud using an analogy from the play of children. In it he advanced the view that children repeat unpleasurable experiences so that they can actively master the situation which they had first experienced passively" (p. 71). Writing about the impulsive trip of an obsessional young man to his birthplace while in analysis, Novey described this person's realization that the environmental features remembered as being of terrifying size—a rock or a valley, for example—were actually small by adult standards. Novey added, "This validation of facts and places I considered not 'acting out' in the sense of acting in the service of not remembering but rather acting which reversed previous avoidance" (p. 86).

Warren Poland (1977) focused on *pilgrimage*, similar to Samuel Novey's concept of *the second look*. Poland wrote that a pilgrimage to places important in one's own history has the goal of mastering internal conflicts, including transgenerational ones. If a pilgrimage takes place when a person is in analysis, it may be a gesture to conceal anxiety and to obviate the need to do difficult emotional work. However, when the traveler has a capacity for introspection, Poland suggested that the person may use the pilgrimage in the service of the ego's integrative function. Agreeing with Poland, I described my own pilgrimage experiences of going back to Cyprus after settling in the United States (Volkan, 1979).

In 1999, Arnold Rothstein stated that the terms *acting out* and *acting in* were less useful to him at that time than they had been thirty years earlier. He referred to a new buzzword in psychoanalytic circles at that time: *enactment*. The term *enactment* was used when the patient's and the analyst's psychologies dovetail to initiate the action. Rothstein wrote: "When I have a new term or a special term I want to know why I need that term. I don't think that we need the term *enactment*. I suggest that the reason we have the term is that we've had a bias against activity which was implicit in the terms *acting out* and *acting in*" (p. 18).

Starting in 1987, I introduced still another term related to our analysands' actions and called it *therapeutic play* (Volkan, 1987, 2010a).

CHAPTER 10

Therapeutic play

In therapeutic play, the "play" is expressed in activities that continue for days or weeks and sometimes much longer. It reflects a story of the patient's key mental conflict with associated pathogenic unconscious fantasies. It becomes the central focus of verbal communication from session to session. As the analysand is involved in actions, he or she tells the analyst about them. The analysand's primary aim of sharing information about activities is not to receive genetic or transference interpretations from the analyst. The patient's primary aim is to crystalize the analyst's image as a "new object" (Loewald, 1960), also known in the psychoanalytic literature as "developmental object" or "analytic introject" (see for example, Baker, 1993; Cameron, 1961; Chused, 1982; Giovacchini, 1972; Kernberg, 1975; Tähkä, 1993; Volkan, 1976). This new image is clearly differentiated from the patient's archaic images that are open or hidden ways displaced onto the analyst as part of transference manifestations. The play comes to an end in a way that is a *new experience* for the analysand, which is shared with a *new object*. After this, the play's meaning for the analysand can be fully brought under psychoanalytic scrutiny.

Before going back to Judy's case, I will now briefly describe another patient's therapeutic play and my becoming a new object for her. Let us call this patient Jennifer. Her total analysis, from its beginning to its end, has been previously published (Volkan, 2010a, 2012). I chose Jennifer's case because she, like Judy, used an animal to search for a solution to her childhood conflicts. The animal she used for her therapeutic play was a horse.

Jennifer's parents were wealthy white people living in the United States who kept alive the racist traditions of the Old South. Jennifer was primarily raised by her African American nanny Sarah who was allowed to live in the basement of the rich people's house. Sarah cooked food for Jennifer, fed her, sang songs to her, hugged and loved her in the basement. The nanny was not allowed to spend time in other parts of the house. When Jennifer was three and a half years old, Sarah was ordered to look after Jennifer's newborn baby sister. She had less time to play with Jennifer, but remained as her primary source for loving care. Nevertheless, Jennifer experienced rejection and loss of love. Jennifer's biological mother treated Jennifer as if she were a beautiful doll, but did not provide good-enough motherly care and love.

The racist tradition provided "two mothers" (Cambor, 1969; Smith, 1949; Volkan & Fowler, 2009) for Jennifer: the biological mother and the black nanny. She escaped much of the necessary childhood psychological work involved in facing both "good" and "bad" aspects of a single mother representation and integrating its opposing images. She experienced early on that when frustrated by one mothering figure, she could seek gratification from the other, all the while hiding the experience with one mother from the experience with the other one. Her corresponding self-representation was also hard to mend. While growing up, Jennifer held on to her white, beautiful doll image, denying the wonderful and warm experiences with the black nanny, especially those before her sister was born. When she, as a young married woman without children, came to see me, she was exhibiting an exaggerated narcissistic personality organization. Her life was full of rituals in which she, as if a beautiful doll, would collect adoration from others.

While in her analysis Jennifer relived her childhood with Sarah through therapeutic play, and experientially learned what she was denying and missing. Then Jennifer mended her self-representation and moved on to go through a normal oedipal development with an integrated self-representation, becoming a happy woman, and, later in her life, a good mother.

After beginning work with her, I learned that Jennifer sometimes would join her rich white friends and go to horse races and horse shows in the Virginia countryside. It was during such an outing that she noticed what she called an "ill-fed" (hungry for love) skinny horse at a stable and got to know Fanny, a black woman who was assigned to take care of this animal. Then her therapeutic play began. She developed a relationship with Fanny and began visiting her almost daily, helping her look after the "hungry" horse.

She used to come to her sessions in splendid dresses and lie on my couch as a "beautiful doll." Now, for a month or so, she was lying on my couch wearing wrinkled jeans. I was waiting for a proper time to be curious with her regarding this change. One day she came in wearing riding clothes. That day for the first time I learned that she was coming from the stables where there was an "ill-fed" horse that she had purchased. The animal now legally belonged to Jennifer and she could still keep it at the same stable. She told me about Fanny, who Jennifer had now hired to look after the horse, and about the intense relationship they were developing.

Listening to her I sensed that the animal represented the part of Jennifer that was hungry for maternal love, and Fanny stood for Sarah. Jennifer went back into action, joining "good" (not rejecting) Sarah in order to have another opportunity to find love. I did not tell Jennifer what came to my mind since I wanted to wait and see how this story would develop. While lying on my couch, Jennifer talked about almost nothing else but how she and Fanny looked after the horse.

After a month or so, I told Jennifer my idea about who the horse and Fanny represented: hungry (for love) child/Jennifer and her nurturing black nanny. She did not respond to my interpretation with any curiosity. She did not verbalize any thoughts or feelings regarding her childhood. Instead, I became a spectator of her outside activities at the stables. Sometimes she came to her sessions wearing dirty jeans and a blouse soiled with animal feces. I wondered to myself if I stood for her white mother who did not know about her loving experiences with Sarah in the basement. Then I sensed that I was a *different* white mother, a "new object/developmental object/analytic object," the nature of which I described above. She wanted me to hear, learn, and appreciate her experiences with a loving black woman without interfering with her activities and without any racist attitudes.

I did not interfere with Jennifer's relationship with her horse and Fanny. I tolerated her describing her actions in detail on my couch four times a week without introducing new topics to wonder about. Her therapeutic play allowed her to have the necessary *crucial juncture* experience during which opposites can come together. She mended the little Jennifers ("love searching" and "doll") and their corresponding white mother and black nanny images.

The term *crucial juncture* was first used by Melanie Klein in 1946. She wrote, "The synthesis between the loved and hated aspects of the complete object gives rise to the feelings of mourning and guilt which imply vital advances in the infant's emotional and intellectual life. This is also a crucial juncture for the choice of neurosis or psychosis" (p. 100). Today we know much more about child development and child–mother interactions in the evolution of the child's mind. However, we are also aware that some individuals do not develop integrated self-representation. Failure to reach a crucial juncture in childhood causes the adult to be stuck in a personality organization in which splitting of self- and object images predominates as a defense.

In discussing the treatment of a patient with a narcissistic personality organization, Otto Kernberg (1970) returned to Melanie Klein's crucial juncture concept. He stated that while treating persons with narcissistic personality organization "the deep admiration and love for the ideal mother" and "the hatred for the distorted dangerous mother" meet in the transference and, at this crucial point, the patient may experience depression and suicidal thoughts "because he has mistreated the analyst and all the significant persons in his life, and he may feel that he has actually destroyed those whom he could have loved and who might have loved him" (p. 81). I described several crucial juncture experiences in my textbook of patients who were undergoing psychoanalytic treatment, including Jennifer's (Volkan, 2010a), and illustrated that no depression or suicidal thoughts accompanied these experiences primarily because the analysts, as "new objects," stood by the patients going through this process.

Jennifer's therapeutic play lasted for nine months. It is beyond the scope of this book to tell the details of Jennifer's analysis after her therapeutic play. Here I will only briefly describe how Jennifer realized becoming a "woman." After the horse was cured, Jennifer began behaving as if she were a tomboy. She began dressing like a man working on a farm, drinking beer with a bunch of young men, both white and African American, listening to their jokes and spending a great deal of time showing her horse to others and entering him in horse shows. Then she learned how to ride her horse. One day she had a dream in which her horse fell as he jumped a fence and bled from his neck. In associating to this dream, she reported how the horse's bleeding enraged her. Soon she came to one of her sessions in extreme puzzlement. In spite of her conscious wish that her animal be protected from injury, she had another dream in which her horse was once more bleeding from his neck. I said to her, "In life, who does bleed regularly?" She looked dumbfounded. After remaining silent for a while she responded: "A woman!"

Now let us return to Judy's case. I already wrote about the meaning of Muri in her life and Dr. Rowan's attempts to explain or interpret this meaning. Judy's actions with her dog during the first year of her analysis were not therapeutic play because Dr. Rowan was not yet a fully developed "new object" in Judy's mind. My task as a supervisor was to help him evolve as a "new object."

Someone who is still studying and learning how to conduct psycho-analysis, as Dr. Rowan was when I began supervising him, expects to notice transference manifestations, their evolutions into workable transference neurosis, and to work through, together with the patient, such developments so as to allow the patient to resolve his or her infantile conflicts. Usually such an expectation and process are written in psychoanalytic literature describing a patient's recovery. Judy's case was not a neurotic case. I sensed that Dr. Rowan was frustrated by Judy's lack of response to his explanations and interpretations of genetic and transference materials. She was not verbalizing deep thoughts and feelings for her analyst. Sometimes Dr. Rowan would feel bored or frustrated and angry. I noticed that working with Judy was making him think that he could not be as good as his classmates. At this phase of Judy's analysis, I knew that I needed to help Dr. Rowan become a "new object" for Judy. As Dr. Rowan's supervisor, I also needed to remain as a "new object" for my supervisee. Dr. Rowan needed to become proud of his psychoanalytic identity, which includes an analyst's ability to hold on to therapeutic neutrality.

CHAPTER 11

Therapeutic neutrality and countertransference

Sigmund Freud mentioned "neutrality" for the first time in 1915 while referring to psychoanalysts' attitude toward their patients. As Axel Hoffer (1985) and Ernest Wallwork (2005) remind us, the German word Freud used for it was "*Indifferenz,*" not "*Neutralitaet,*" the actual word for "neutrality." While translating Freud's works into English, James Strachey used the word "neutrality," thereafter replacing "indifference" as the term accepted in the English psychoanalytic literature. Freud's different comments about this term do not provide a clear-cut understanding of what he meant by it (Moore & Fine, 1990). His best description of this term, I think, took place when he wrote that analysts should avoid turning a patient seeking our help "into our private property, to decide his fate for him, to force our own ideals on him, and with the pride of a Creator to form him in our own image and to see that it is good" (Freud, 1919a, p. 164).

Throughout decades, many psychoanalysts from different "schools" of psychoanalysis have discussed what Freud meant by neutrality. (For a review of the literature on this see Volkan, 2019.) Burness Moore and Bernard Fine's (1990) description of neutrality links it to countertransference: "Central to psychoanalytic neutrality are keeping the countertransference in check, avoiding the imposition of one's own values upon the patient, and taking the patient's capacities rather than one's own desires as a guide .... The analyst's neutrality is intended to facilitate the development, recognition, and interpretation of the transference neurosis and to minimize distortions that might be introduced if he or she attempts to educate, advise, or impose values upon the patient based on the analyst's countertransference" (p. 127). I believe that today most analysts, including me, agree with this definition. I should add that Dr. Rowan's neutrality was crucial in allowing his patient to perceive him as a "new object."

There are certain interferences by an analyst that should not be considered as giving up neutrality. I do not consider an analyst's interference with a patient's behavior *within* the analytic office that prevents therapeutic engagement to indicate that this analyst is not remaining neutral. Let us go back to Rebecca's case. As I wrote earlier, as soon as she started her analysis she would put a Life Saver candy in her mouth before lying on my couch. I recall saying something like this to her: "Your having a Life Saver in your mouth has a meaning. We will be curious about this. Since no one taught me how to work with an analysand while she keeps something in her mouth, your analysis will *not* start until the time when you will not hide something in your mouth. I am not ordering you to get rid of your candy right away. I will wait until you are in my room with me without a Life Saver in your mouth." As I wrote earlier, a few weeks later Rebecca began her analytic sessions without her Life Saver.

Judy bought her puppy before her analysis started. It was an action *outside* of her analyst's office. It took some time for Dr. Rowan and I to notice the primary reason for her relationship with Muri. Judy freely talked about this relationship and shared her pet experiences with her analyst. We did not even imagine telling Judy to get rid of Muri, since we sensed that her relationship with the puppy was her way of seeking a solution for her hunger for a libidinal object. She would hear her analyst's remarks about this relationship even though she was not yet ready to see Muri as just a pet. Unlike what I had done with Rebecca, Dr. Rowan's suggestion to his analysand to give up her dog would have been his giving up his psychoanalytic neutrality.

On rare occasions a psychoanalyst faces realistic reasons for giving up neutrality. Here are two examples.

A young woman in analysis named Pattie had a history of sexual abuse by her father. When she was a small child, her mother suffered from depression and her father turned his attentions towards his daughter. When she reached puberty, her father saw her menstrual blood and, for some reason, this ended his abuse of his daughter. During the latter part of her analysis, while she was reliving her childhood trauma in her transference, the patient began imagining that it was dangerous for her to park her car in the parking lot near my office. She had been using this parking lot without any complaints for more than three years. She had recently seen a man in the parking lot and had developed a strong fear that he might sexually assault her. The sexually abusing father's image in the transference had been taken out of my office and externalized onto this man. The patient became very anxious. I was still waiting for her to relive fully her childhood trauma and then work through it.

One day Pattie came in with a big handbag, lay down on my couch, firmly holding the bag with both hands and said: "I decided to protect myself from the man I saw in the parking lot. I brought a loaded pistol with me. It is in my handbag." I spontaneously responded: "One anxious person in this room is enough. I do not wish to be anxious. Now you get up and leave my office. Get rid of your loaded pistol and then come back." Also, I added: "If you use a gun and then go to jail, I want you to know that no one taught me how to conduct analysis in a jail." After a minute or so the patient got up and left the room. I kept the door slightly ajar. The patient returned about ten minutes before the conclusion of her session, closed the door and lay down on my couch.

Another patient, this one a young man, in the first year of his analysis, developed intense curiosity about my everyday life. Here I will not describe his psychological reasons for this. Without telling me, he found out that I am married and where we lived. He began parking in front of my home and following my wife when she went out. If she went to the grocery store, he would be standing behind her at the checkout. My wife noticed she was being followed. When my patient told me that he was the one following her, I said: "What we do here is between you and me. If you follow my wife even one more time, I will stop being your analyst and I will call the police." He never bothered my wife again, and three years later he completed his analysis.

Decades ago, it was easier for an analyst to keep his or her personal life private. In today's world, with incredible communication technology, by simply opening a computer, patients can find information about their analysts on the internet. When I conduct supervision, I advise younger analysts not to include personal data on social media. As I am writing this book, the Covid-19 pandemic has forced psychoanalysts to conduct analysis via telephone or telecommunication. Both the analyst and the analysand are facing the same unseen enemy. I (Volkan, 2020, pp. 135–136) already briefly described analysands' and analysts' initial responses to this situation. Jerome Blackman (2020), derived from his experience while teaching and supervising dynamic therapists in China, presented data on the psychological effects of Covid-19 in Wuhan, apparently where this pandemic began in December 2019. I am sure that at a later date there will be papers or books on how this pandemic has affected psychoanalytic neutrality.

CHAPTER 12

Reaching P and renovating a new house

S oon after buying Muri, Judy noticed a young man at the dog park strolling with his girlfriend. She liked the young man's looks and started talking with him and his girlfriend. The first letter of this young man's first name is the letter A. Let us call him Albert. Judy right away was aware that Albert was much younger than she. Later she would learn that in fact Albert was more than eight years younger.

When she met Albert alone at the dog park a few days later, she decided to "hunt" him, and invited him to her apartment. First she briefly considered not having sex with him since he was much younger, but she ended up going to bed with Albert. During one of her psychoanalytic sessions she described her need to have sex with Albert in the following way: "I felt like a very hungry person who would eat anything, even though I knew that what I would take in would have no nutritional value. Whom I hunt has zero nutritional value. My need to hunt and have sex with Albert or someone else is also like an urgent feeling, like needing to go to the bathroom right away and empty my bowels. Then I leave that person and hunt another one." A follower of Sigmund Freud very easily will note the contamination of Judy's sexual addiction with oral and anal issues, her need for oral satisfaction and her need to get rid of food without nutritional value and accompanied by her anger.

Dr. Rowan and I noticed that Judy would not leave Albert. She continued hunting him whenever his girlfriend was not around. Then we noticed that she was using Albert in the same way she was relating to Muri. Most of the time, younger Albert would represent the love-hungry little Judy, and by being with him she would test if a mother's taking good care of her child is a possibility. At the same time, she continued to have relationships with other men too, but now without the urgency of her previous sexual addiction.

Toward the end of the first year of her analysis, Judy took another overseas trip, this time to Singapore and Hong Kong. During her trip, she dreamed she was a passenger on a plane that crashed and every passenger, except Judy, died. She was left alone. Dr. Rowan summarized how Judy's separating from her analyst once more reminded her of the many separations and the loneliness she had experienced in her childhood. Dr. Rowan repeated that with A, B, and C she was still testing with actions to see if the loving care she had missed in her childhood could be available for her. Once more he mentioned that he was R who had not gone away and who was a steady person.

Dr. Rowan and I became aware that the names of all the men Judy was having relationships with at that time started with the letter A. What was interesting was Judy's own awareness of this. She was far away from R. Besides talking about Albert, her calling him or having sex with him whenever she felt lonely, she was making references to relationships with Alfred, Adler, and Adam.

We learned that the name of the cousin who molested her when she was five or six years old also started with A. Talking about this cousin, she "remembered" his trying to put his penis in her mouth. She was not sure if this recollection was real or not. I told Dr. Rowan to inquire if Judy had a habit of performing fellatio on the men she had hunted and was hunting. Then I sensed that Dr. Rowan, most likely due to coming from a conservative family, had been shy and hesitant to speak with his patient openly about the details of her physical sexual acts. But since I could do so, now Dr. Rowan could also do so.

We learned that when involved in physical sexual activity, Judy was using her vagina as a mouth to receive "food" for her hunger, not her mouth. But her relating to Albert, outside of their being involved in physical sexual activities, was very much connected with her mouth.

"Every time I see Albert food comes to my mind," she would say on the couch. "Every time we are together, we eat something." She also described how she had taught Muri to carry a toy in her mouth. When this topic came up, she and Dr. Rowan easily connected it with little Judy's need for a pacifier in her mouth until she started attending elementary school.

After returning from the Far East, Judy sold her car and bought a used one with more space in it for Muri. She thought of taking Muri to the very busy downtown area of her city. Once more, through action, as she stated, she wanted "to teach Muri how to learn to socialize."

Soon she revisited her molestation, also with an action. She met a man whose name also started with A. She checked him out on the internet and found that he was someone who liked to look at pornography and view naked women. One day she missed coming to her psychoanalytic session and instead met this man. First they talked about oral sex and kissed. Then they went to a movie theater and sat in the back row. She called this location in the theater "a place where you find seats for lovers." After the lights went off and the movie started, as she expected, the man began touching her legs. Then he took his penis out and, by grasping Judy's hand, he made her touch it. Judy described how, at first, she could not move her hand away from this man's penis. She knew that in the past she had undergone a similar experience. "This time, however, I was able to put a stop to it," she added, and she refused to participate any further in sexual acts in the movie theatre. Also, she did not date this man again. She was aware that she wanted to remember her having been molested, not by talking, but through an action. She wanted to see if this time she could protect herself.

As the second year of her analysis continued, Judy started to introduce her new men to Dr. Rowan by saying, "Now let me tell you about B," or, "Let me introduce you to K." We noticed that she would not hunt a man whose name started with R or any letter in the alphabet that came after R. I sensed that she would not find R until she was sure that R was a much different object—a "new object"—than the men she was hunting in her repeated search for good maternal/paternal care.

I noted how her search for a "new object" in Dr. Rowan, as well as her doubts about him, were being expressed during her sessions. Often, especially after Dr. Rowan made a linking interpretation and connected a current event's theme with a theme from her childhood, Judy would say:

"What is the use of making these connections? I know them anyhow," and then she would add "Mr. Doctor," or "Mr. Psychologist," or "Mr. Mental Health Worker," to finish her sentence in spite of her knowing that Dr. Rowan was a psychiatrist and he was conducting psychoanalysis with her. Indirectly, she was belittling Dr. Rowan, making him also a plate of food without nutrition.

Such name-calling, I sensed, would induce frustration and anger in Dr. Rowan. But more importantly, I sensed that Judy was making him think that he had not yet become a good enough psychoanalyst. As a supervisor I told Dr. Rowan: "Judy is not doing this because of your blue eyes." Several times I gently explained Judy's need to test him again and again to find out if he could become and remain a steady "new object." I was very satisfied to notice that soon Dr. Rowan's frustrations disappeared. I saw with pleasure that he was developing a solid psychoanalytic identity. Every time Judy called him "Mr. Doctor," or "Mr. Psychologist," or "Mr. Mental Health Worker," he reminded his patient that none of these titles reflected his role in her life and that she was still struggling to accept him as a steady object.

As months passed, Judy introduced P to her analytic sessions. At that time, once more she had stopped hunting men for a couple of months. Instead, she had started to drink alcohol more than she had done before. She came to a Monday session and said the following: "Last Friday my boss at work gave me a task. I was asked to evaluate a person who had applied for a position at our firm. After interviewing this person, I recommended against giving the position to him. I had learned that he had problems. Then I had a difficult weekend, most likely due to my knowing that I also have problems and I cannot leave them behind. Then I thought about a man l had seen recently. What a handsome man! Testosterone is leaking out of his body! I drank a lot and went to a restaurant. I knew that this man—his name is Paul—would be there. I met P there. I needed someone to cuddle me. So I invited P to my apartment. But somehow we ended up in his hotel room. Next morning I left him without having breakfast with him. I added P to our alphabet, Mr. Mental Health Therapist. I am introducing you to P. Yesterday I wanted to call Albert. But I did not. I am still a turtle. I hope that I will give up being a turtle. Last night I had a dream about a turtle."

Then Judy reported her dream in which she first saw a ship in the sea. A storm was coming. A world-engulfing flood would take place. She realized that the ship was Noah's Ark. God would spare people and animals on Noah's Ark. She, her parents, her brother, and her brother's wife and son were standing at the shore. Her brother's little boy threw a rope towards Noah's Ark and the rope became tied to the ship. Judy said: "The boy appears as if he is very strong and pulls Noah's Ark towards us so that we, our family, can also enter it and be saved. But suddenly what he is pulling turns into a turtle; Noah's Ark disappears. The rope is pulling this turtle to the shore. I want the turtle to land in a safe place, away from the stormy sea. But an eagle sits on the turtle. The turtle cannot get out of the stormy sea. What do you think about my dream, Mr. Doctor?"

Dr. Rowan reminded Judy that a week earlier, in another dream, she saw an eagle picking up a baby and taking the baby up in the sky. In the dream, Judy had wondered if the eagle was going to save or drop the baby and injure or kill him. Dr. Rowan continued: "Today, once more, you called me Mr. Mental Health Therapist and Mr. Doctor. You want me to be trustworthy, but you are still wondering if I could be and stay trustworthy. Last week you described a picture of many animals together, like many animals in Noah's Ark that you described today. Last week, after you visualized many animals, you had another picture in your mind in which a butcher was holding a sharp knife. You had wondered if the butcher was going to cut up the animals. The way the butcher was holding the knife reminded you of your father's arm raised to slap you. We have discussed many times your search through your different actions for someone who could be trusted and who would provide real care and love and no punishment. Many times I've told you that I am R who has been standing by you. Now you are introducing P to me. What letter comes in the alphabet after P? R comes after P. I want to remind you again that I am not Mr. Mental Health Therapist or Mr. Doctor."

During the latter part of the second year of her analysis, Judy became preoccupied with finding a new house. Dr. Rowan told her that her preoccupation was also related to her finding a new house within herself. He added that he would continue working with her as she made changes within herself, as she changed the deprived-child image. He did not interfere with Judy's search for a new place in the external world.

There was no difficulty on Judy's part in agreeing with Dr. Rowan that what she really wanted was a new internal structure in her core self. This did not stop her from searching for a house in an obsessional way without expressing curiosity about her psychological wishes and fantasies. Once more she was using "actions"; this time she was "hunting" for a new home and also learning how to deal with realtors. She was also hoping that Muri would be happier in a bigger place with a garden.

Judy looked at a house which was very near to her brother's house. When he became aware of this, he told Judy not to move near where he and his family were living because of Judy's "bad habits" with men; neighbors noticing his sister collecting men with one-night stands would embarrass him and his wife. Her brother's wife was pregnant again; later, little twin sisters would be added to their family. On the couch, Judy would not say much about the newborn twins. Her realization of losing "twinning" with her brother was settling in Judy's mind. Her obsession with searching for a new house and talking about it on the couch continued.

Many months later, Judy bought a house at a location away from the district where her brother and his family were living. Right away, she hired workers to renovate the house and paint the inside and outside walls white. She asked Dr. Rowan to explain to her again "what is remembering with actions?" Then she continued to verbalize how she knew that the physical changes she was determined to make to the appearance of her new house were her attempts to be a new woman who would be cleansed of her hunting symptoms; her psychological dirt would be covered with white paint. "I want a new bed," she declared, and added that she would not bring men to her new place for one-night stands. She was successful for about eight months.

She had a dream in that she screamed at her mother, and told her to "get out of my life!" On the couch she recalled how her mother often told lies when Judy was a child, implying that her daughter had done something wrong. Hearing this, her father sometimes would beat little Judy. She recalled how her mother had given a gift to a teacher, even though she knew that this teacher had been mean to Judy's brother.

After not having a man in her house for eight months, Judy's hunting men restarted, in a slow fashion. She would bring some men to her new location.

CHAPTER 13

Finding R

As her psychoanalysis continued, Dr. Rowan and I noted another meaning in Judy's relationship with her analyst. Now Judy started to come late to her sessions and sometimes to "forget" to show up, making Dr. Rowan sit alone waiting for her. Judy was externalizing her hungry rejected childhood image onto her analyst to see if a "hungry for love" person could tolerate this situation, leave this image behind, and develop a more advanced and comfortable personality organization. Transference manifestations of persons with preoedipal conflicts can be very frustrating. Once more, supervision included helping Dr. Rowan to know and feel that Judy's frustrating behavior was not due to Dr. Rowan's blue eyes.

Judy's efforts toward finding a caring libidinal object were also accompanied by her repeating stories and dreams, illustrating a wish to actualize a "new beginning" (Balint, 1932, 1959) or a rebirth (Rose, 1969). Many analysands with neurotic or lower-level personality organization report stories and dreams reflecting their hope for a therapeutic progression following a therapeutic regression accompanied by a change in their psychological structure—their giving up a defensive behavior pattern and developing a more adaptive one. They illustrate such wishes or accomplishments with a fantasy of being born again. The reader will recall that Jennifer's taking care of a sick horse with the help of Fanny took nine months. After nine months, Jennifer was "reborn."

Judy's buying a new house, renovating it, and also not hunting men for eight months reflected a new beginning for her, but she could not maintain this change. As her dreams symbolically illustrated, she was still stuck in a lake or sea. Elsewhere I presented stories of other analysands who had very similar dreams (Volkan, 2010a). When these analysands resolved their conflicts, they reported dreams in which they could swim to shore, stand up, and be safe. Here is a brief example.

Peter was much traumatized in early childhood. His father left the family when his son was only a few months old. Peter's mother overfed him and he became an obese child. A new man came into his life, marrying his mother, becoming his stepfather and also his main caregiver. This man was suffering from extreme war trauma. He had experienced the Bataan Death March and time as a prisoner of war. When Peter was in his early teens, the stepfather introduced Peter to guns and taught him how to hunt. For the stepfather, to be a hunter and not a hunted one was a crucial psychological need. The stepfather's relationship with Peter created a hunter image in his stepson. Adult Peter, after experiencing an event that would make him feel anxious, would kill dozens of deer by machine-gunning them from a helicopter. He was an animal killer. In his mid-forties he sought psychoanalytic treatment because he had a superiority complex accompanied by severe marital problems, bulimia, and drinking issues.

I describe Peter's analysis from its beginning to its termination in my book *Animal Killer: Transmission of War Trauma from One Generation to the Next* (Volkan, 2014). Here I will focus on his repeating dream throughout his analysis in which he saw himself walking on water like Jesus Christ. Toward the termination phase of his analysis, after his internal world had changed, he began to have new versions of this recurring dream. First, he was not walking on water but on a submarine that was lying a few inches below the surface of the water. He realized that the submarine stood for his stepfather who had worked on a submarine just before the Japanese captured him. This new version of his recurring dream gave Peter firm insight that the stepfather supported his omnipotent "hunter" self-image. Then Peter had another version of his recurring dream. In this one, the submarine dove, and Peter fell into the water. He could then swim to shore as an "average" individual. He had a new "birth."

Judy, in her dreams, was still in a lake wanting to climb a tree in the middle of it. If she achieved this, she would still be away from other human beings since the tree was surrounded by water. In her recurring dreams she could not succeed in reaching the tree. Several times she told Dr. Rowan that a plant in his office looked like the tree in her dreams. Then she would state that Dr. Rowan was not taking good care of his plant and that the leaves of the plant were dry.

One day, instead of taking Muri to the dog park, she took him to a forest outside her city. Suddenly she realized that a tree in this forest looked like the tree in the middle of the water in her dreams. She touched it. She thought that finding the tree in her dream now had become a *reality* and it was not in the middle of a lake.

Soon she also found a man whose name started with R. On the couch she kept referring to R's habits. Apparently, after being with Judy in her bedroom, R always wanted to open the bedroom windows for fresh air and to look outside and enjoy the environment surrounding Judy's house, a wider world. After staying with R for a month, Judy, on the couch, repeatedly asked: "I have been with him for a month; why doesn't R tell me that he loves me?" One day, while having sex with R, she felt pain in her vagina. Soon afterwards, by accident, she saw R in the street walking and holding hands with a woman Judy did not know. She ended her relationship with R. Dr. Rowan told Judy the following: "In the past we talked about A, B, C and I referred to myself as R. At this time, referring to myself as R would be a *mistake*. Therefore, I want to make a correction. I am not R, I am Rowan."

After this session, there was a big change in Judy's attitude toward her analyst. For the first time in her analysis, she began wondering if Dr. Rowan was married or not: "I think you are married; I think you have a child." She added, "I know that we cannot marry," and then described how she wanted to be married and have a child. We noticed that Judy did not develop an open erotic transference toward Dr. Rowan. A girlfriend told Judy to get pregnant while she was in her thirties and not to wait until her forties. Judy went through an egg freezing procedure, leaving the option of pursuing motherhood to a later time.

Judy recalled how, at the beginning of her work with Dr. Rowan, he had wondered if she was inquiring about the backgrounds of men before sleeping with them—who they were, what their interests might be, and so on. Now Judy began looking at online dating sites to find men and tried to learn about them before actually meeting them. For a while she chose to date men who were divorced and who had children, but would not openly connect their images with her image of her analyst. But, she reported that what Dr. Rowan and she discussed during her sessions would come to her mind when she met new people, when she searched for food, when she wanted to drink alcohol, and even when she had an urge to play with Muri. It was now clear that she was keeping Dr. Rowan as an "analytic introject" in her mind.

Dr. Rowan was careful not to sound as if he were ordering Judy to do this or that, or turning the analytic introject into a severe superego. Here is an example.

One day on the couch, Judy talked about finding a potential date on the internet and then learning that this man had a history of substance abuse. Judy reported that at this moment Dr. Rowan came to her mind. The next day on the couch, she wondered if Dr. Rowan would allow her to be with this man. Instead of expressing his opinion, Dr. Rowan stated that his analysand had made a change, and now she was taking into consideration the realities of the world. He added that Judy, at her workplace, was capable of evaluating realities while she was carrying out her responsibilities. Therefore, her checking on realities in regard to dating men was also available to her. She was the one who had found the man's long history with drug abuse; she was the one who considered, in fact she knew, that this man would not be suitable for dating.

Then we heard an interesting observation on Judy's part. She noticed that when she gave up an old habit, this would often be followed by a bout of diarrhea. Following this, I had a discussion with Dr. Rowan about the mourning process after a significant loss and how children do not know how to mourn as adults and have no name for their reactions to losses (Furman, 1974; Volkan, 1981; Volkan & Zintl, 1993). We wondered if Judy's diarrhea was her way of mourning, letting go of unwanted images through a bodily reaction. We decided that Dr. Rowan, during one of his upcoming sessions with Judy, would name her bodily reaction as "mourning" and explain how mourning the loss of people and things, including old habits, induces freedom for trying out new relationships.

Judy continued to see Albert now and then and sometimes Paul. Her pathological hunting behavior was gone. Then she found another man who was another R. This time, before sleeping with him, she spent time finding out who he was and shared this information with Dr. Rowan. Her relationship with this second R was short lived. She had a dream in which once more she was lost in the sea. This time, she saw no tree. Instead, she found a boat and got into it. She knew that she was safe, but still lonely. She did not yet attempt to go to shore.

Meanwhile, I was noticing with pleasure how Dr. Rowan had become a colleague with a strong psychoanalytic identity. In a session with Judy, Dr. Rowan made a detailed summary illustrating his analysand's transference expressions and his counter-responses to them. He verbalized where Judy was in her analysis and what she and her analyst would need to work on going forward. He told me that he focused on three issues. The first two issues were directly related to Judy's transference.

In the first, Dr. Rowan reminded Judy that she, as a child, felt deprived of maternal and paternal care and now her childhood experiences were being repeated *between them*. But in this repetition, he was the deprived child whenever she came ten to twenty minutes late to her sessions and whenever she forgot to come at all. Judy was remembering her childhood self with a new type of action, now taking place between her and her analyst. Sometimes he felt discomfort and even anger when Judy ignored him and her sessions. But he never gave up his knowledge that such feelings really belonged to his analysand and that his sensing them allowed him to know what little Judy had gone through. He reminded Judy that he was always present for her sessions and added, "Stopping this habit of making me a deprived child will be a new experience for you. This will allow you to have a life without constantly being bothered by a deprived child image. This is one issue we will work on and you will stop coming late to your sessions or forgetting them." Dr. Rowan added that he knew the reality and the necessity of her visits to other countries to be part of her work, and he was not referring to these absences.

Dr. Rowan referred to Judy's second habit in her relationship with her analyst: her calling him "Mr. Doctor," or "Mr. Psychologist," or

"Mr. Mental Health Worker," in spite of knowing his real professional identity. Dr. Rowan added that in the past, most of the time, she did not know A, B, or C's personalities, who they were before dating them. Therefore, unconsciously, she behaved as if they would be "good lovers," while knowing that they would turn out to be like food without nutrition. She would be disappointed. Dr. Rowan noted that Judy wanted to know where the second R was born, what his politics were, what songs he liked, and so on. Dr. Rowan added: "Your curiosity and attempts to learn about realities in current relationships is a big change. Not every relationship is a repetition of your childhood relationships. I do not tell you about my personal life, but I know that you got to know who I am in this office. Together we will follow this development and work on your not giving me titles that do not belong to me."

After speaking about Judy's transference manifestations, in his summary, Dr. Rowan referred to Judy's twinning with her brother without using the technical term and then added: "Your brother's wife gave birth to twin sisters. You perceived and experienced this as another piece of evidence that your old relationship with your brother is now lost. Following this, you had a symptom; you thought that a bad odor was coming from your vagina. You visited a gynecologist and found out that nothing is wrong with your vagina. Remember how we have discussed your using your vagina as your mouth. I think that you wished to find out if your mouth is functional and clean. Now we will look closely at you not using your vagina as a mouth."

Then Dr. Rowan told Judy that he could see that his analysand was already working on this, wanting to know what she was putting in her mouth and what she was going to eat. He said: "You began investigating men, finding out about their backgrounds, their societal activities, political inclinations. You stopped having sex with everyone you date. Your hunting behavior is gone; you are no longer an ant or a turtle. When men stop being food without nutrition, your vagina stops being a mouth."

Then Dr. Rowan added that he was clearly hearing Judy's wishes for her future, her wanting to be a secure woman and a mother. He finished his summary by stating, "I focused on your two habits in my office and a change in your dealing with men. I presented a summary of where we are." Judy agreed with her analyst.

Around this time, Dr. Rowan completed his psychoanalytic training and officially became a psychoanalyst. He and I met at a meeting where Dr. Rowan presented a paper. I listened to his presentation and was impressed with his description of resolving transference-countertransference issues in the treatment of another patient. When we met alone and talked about his work with Judy, Dr. Rowan thanked me for my help and showed genuine appreciation of my role in his developing a psychoanalytic identity. He also stated that he did not need further supervision. I went along with his request, and my weekly telephone supervision of Dr. Rowan came to an end.

CHAPTER 14

What happened to Judy after I stopped working with Dr. Rowan?

During a psychoanalytic gathering, I was asked unexpectedly to join in a discussion on the psychology of individuals with addictions. I realized that Judy's case had been the best teaching case, demonstrating why and how an individual develops a non-chemical addition. This initiated my motivation to write this book with the four aims I mentioned in my introductory chapter. After I completed the first thirteen chapters, I sent an email to Dr. Rowan and asked him to fill me in about his continuing work with Judy after my supervisory work with him had ended over two years ago. He answered right away and expressed his surprise that he had received my email on the day of Judy's marriage. What a coincidence! Dr. Rowan was expecting a call from Judy, the first as a married woman, two days before she would leave for her honeymoon and he had planned to get in touch with me after talking to her to inform me about this big change in her life.

A few weeks later, Dr. Rowan and I talked on the phone and I received detailed information about the last two years of Judy's analysis. Around the time when my supervision of Dr. Rowan ended, Judy had no urgency to meet a man. Her sexual addiction was gone. As I stated earlier, Judy had started to find dates on the internet. She would try to get as much information as possible about a future date before contacting him, and would only meet with a man when she thought there was potential for a long and hopefully lasting relationship. Dr. Rowan noticed that Judy's interest in married or divorced men with children continued after she told her analyst that she thought of him as married with children. Still, there was no evolution of an open erotic transference.

One day while visiting her dentist, Judy mentioned that she had been undergoing psychoanalysis. Her dentist asked who her analyst was. Upon hearing Dr. Rowan's name, the dentist told her that his wife and Dr. Rowan's wife were best friends. This was the first time Judy learned that in fact her analyst was a married man. Recalling Dr. Rowan's remarks that she knew who he was from her visits with him in his office, she quickly told her dentist not to tell her anything else about Dr. Rowan and his family life. She added: "I keep the nature of my relationship with my analyst between us; it is better that I do not hear about his life outside his office." While on the couch, Judy had stopped calling Dr. Rowan "Mr. Doctor," or "Mr. Psychologist," or "Mr. Mental Health Worker." She continued to come late to some of her sessions, but with an open awareness of the meaning of this gesture.

I learned that Judy had found her future husband on an internet dating site two years before they were married. Let us call him Mathew. Reading about him, she noticed that Mathew was a few years older than she and had a steady business, which required him to travel to other locations, like Judy's father had done and as Judy was still doing. She sensed that Mathew was an intelligent person with a good sense of humor. When she got in touch with Mathew she learned that recently he had been in a car accident and was still having difficulty walking.

She started dating Mathew and, in a sense, began taking care of him. She drove him around since, due to his injury he could not do so himself at that time. She would take him to restaurants; they would sit together and talk and get to know each other. She realized that Mathew was a serious, dependable, and financially very secure person.

Her looking after Mathew took nearly a year as he slowly became well and healthy again. They were also lovers, talking about having a future together. She liked being with him. She said, "I love him and he loves me. He is a dependable and responsible person. He also enjoys Muri."

After Mathew returned to full health, he and Judy became engaged, but Judy kept postponing the wedding date. According to Judy, her fiancé did not want to have children, while she insisted that she was determined to be a mother. She would not marry Mathew until he would agree to have a child or children with her.

After meeting Mathew, Judy never dated any other man. She did not say anything to Mathew about her past as a hunter of men. Her sexual addiction remained a private memory. Paul was living in another location in the United States, and once he returned to Judy's city for a short visit. They met for lunch, but did not have sex. Mathew knew that Judy had spent time with a male visitor and he asked her if she had gone to bed with this visitor in the past. On the couch, Judy stated that she did not wish to tell a lie to her fiancé. On the other hand, she did not wish to hurt Mathew. So, she told him it would be best for both of them to keep some very personal issues from their past to themselves. Mathew went along with this.

Judy made another major change in her life. She quit her prestigious job and started her own consultation business, which included communicating with many organizations in different countries. She already knew that she would be successful. Her new responsibilities allowed her to work at home on the computer. After Mathew agreed to have a child or children with Judy, he sold his house and moved in with her a little over four months before their wedding date.

Two months later the Covid-19 pandemic became the unseen enemy of humankind. Dr. Rowan was still seeing his patients in person when Judy told him that, in order to protect herself and Mathew, she would not come to the office. They began to have sessions using the internet, seeing each other at the beginning and the end of the sessions. During the rest of the session, Dr. Rowan would watch Judy lying on a couch in her house and listen to her. Soon Judy asked to give up this way of getting together, and she began to reach Dr. Rowan by telephone, without missing any of her sessions.

Elsewhere I wrote briefly about sixteen analysands' initial responses to the Covid-19 pandemic and stated that one common response was their returning to their childhood losses and re-experiencing anxieties and old defense mechanisms and fantasies linked to such losses (Volkan, 2020). In Judy's case, as I understood it, there was no expression of overwhelming anxiety. She did not return to her childhood losses. At home, Mathew would settle next to Judy in front of his computer, and they would take care of their businesses side by side, talk, and experience togetherness. In her case the Covid-19 pandemic, in a sense, was helpful for her as it created a situation of togetherness with the same man and helped her develop a deeper relationship with him.

I understood that before the wedding, Judy "visited" her twinning relationship with her brother; most likely to say goodbye to it. One day on the phone she described how during the previous hours she was having a good time with Mathew at home, working next to him. Apparently, Mathew is someone who likes to tell jokes and laughs a lot. When Mathew told a new joke on that day and started laughing, Judy suddenly thought of her brother. In the past, she would call her brother and tell him about men she had hunted. Now she thought of telling her brother about Mathew and his habit of telling jokes. She wondered if her brother would approve or not approve of Mathew's behavior. As soon as Judy reported this, both Dr. Rowan and Judy also verbalized how her old habit with her brother was gone; she was responsible for her own relationship with Mathew.

Judy and Mathew did not postpone their wedding. They had paid for a big wedding ceremony, but the realities of the virus pandemic forced them to marry in the garden of Mathew's brother's big house. Only some family members, keeping social distance, were present. Judy's parents managed to come to her wedding, as did her brother and his family.

I asked Dr. Rowan about Albert and Muri. Apparently, during the last two years, his analysand had not talked much about either Albert or Muri. Albert was now married and no longer a part of Judy's life. Dr. Rowan told me that during the last two years on the couch, his analysand once compared having sex with Mathew with having sex with Albert. She stated that physical aspects of sex were more exciting with the younger Albert, but now what she had found with Mathew was a very different kind of satisfaction. She added, "Albert was not a romantic person."

I learned that just before her marriage ceremony, Judy had a dream. In the dream, she knew that her dog would be stolen but she did not feel bad knowing that Muri would be gone from her life. I thought that Muri now was only a dog, no longer an important symbol for the analysand, a reservoir for her externalizations.

Judy and Mathew rented a place near a beach for their honeymoon. I learned that they had taken Muri with them to this beach resort. After arriving, they were informed that no dogs were allowed to run on the beach, even though it was rather empty because of the virus pandemic. It was Mathew who took Muri for walks on a leash.

As the reader can imagine, I wondered why Judy had spent almost a year dating and taking care of a man who had been injured in a car accident, staying with him and then marrying him. In her relationship with Muri and Albert she was trying to find out if a relationship between a loving mother and cared-for child could exist. In the transference, she had made Dr. Rowan the rejected child by not coming to or forgetting her sessions. These issues were very much explored during her analysis.

To my great surprise, Dr. Rowan shared new information that had never come up while I was his supervisor. Dr. Rowan wanted me to know how Judy's choosing Mathew might also have connections with Judy's transference feelings for him. I learned that two years before he started seeing Judy face to face in once-a-week psychotherapy, Dr. Rowan had a liver problem. He was given a new medicine, which had caused severe side effects such as his losing weight and feeling very weak. Eventually, he became a completely well person, but he told me that when he started working with Judy, most likely she had sensed his physical difficulties. I recalled seeing seeing Dr. Rowan at a meeting after the first year of my being his supervisor and perceiving him as a rather skinny individual. When I saw him three years later, just before my work with him ended, Dr. Rowan's physical appearance reflected health. Dr. Rowan also volunteered to describe how when he was a child, he was in an accident in which his leg was broken and he had to stay in bed for three and a half months. He would completely recover after a year. He added: "Of course, Judy does not know this."

I learned that Judy did not yet wish to terminate her analysis. She and Mathew decided to wait for three or four months after their marriage before she would be ready to become pregnant. She shared this news with her analyst. Furthermore, she wanted to see him again for analytic sessions face to face when they no longer had to be separated by the Covid-19 pandemic.

I asked myself if Judy, through her interactions with Mathew, unconsciously linked his injured image to Dr. Rowan's image when he was recovering from his illness. In any case she had found out that taking care of an injured someone and making this someone healthy and happy can actually happen. Her constant search for "love," which would turn out to be like food without nutrition, had gone. I realized that Dr. Rowan's work with Judy was successful.

Above I wrote about how Judy's initial response to the **Covid**-19 pandemic seemed to be helpful in deepening her relationship with Mathew. I must add that I also felt sad that soon after becoming an emotionally healthy woman, Judy, like her analyst, his supervisor, and other human beings, would be exposed to the real dangers of this pandemic, even though she was no longer alone.

References

Abt, L., & Weissman, S. (1965). *Acting Out: Theoretical and Clinical Aspects.* New York: Grune & Stratton.

Ainslie, R. (1997). *The Psychology of Twinship.* Northvale, NJ: Jason Aronson.

Akhtar, S. (2009). *Comprehensive Dictionary of Psychoanalysis.* London: Karnac.

Akhtar, S., & Volkan, V. D. (Eds.) (2005a). *Mental Zoo: Animals in the Human Mind and Its Pathology.* New York: International Universities Press.

Akhtar, S., & Volkan, V. D. (Eds.) (2005b). *Cultural Zoo: Animals in the Human Mind and Its Sublimations.* New York: International Universities Press.

Atik, F. (2019). *A Psychoanalyst on His Own Couch: A Biography of Vamık Volkan and His Psychoanalytic and Psychopolitical Concepts.* Bicester, UK: Phoenix.

Bach, S. (1977). On the narcissistic state of consciousness. *International Journal of Psychoanalysis, 58:* 209–233.

Bagot, R. C., Zhang, T. Y., Wen, X., Nguyen, T. T., Nguyen, H. B., Diorio, J., Wong, T. P., & Meaney, M. J. (2012). Variations in postnatal maternal care and the epigenetic regulation of metabotropic glutamate receptor 1 expression and hippocampal function in the rat. *Proceedings of the National Academy of Sciences U S A - Supplement, 109:* 17200–17207.

Baker, R. (1993). The patient's discovery of the analyst as a new object. *International Journal of Psychoanalysis, 74:* 1223–1233.

Balint, M. (1932). *Primary Love and Psychoanalytic Technique* (pp. 33–35). London: Tavistock.

Balint, M. (1959). *Thrills and Regression.* London: Hogarth.

Berg, M. D. (1977). Externalizing transference. *International Journal of Psychoanalysis, 58*: 235–244.

Bion, W. R. (1950). *Second Thoughts*. London: Karnac.

Blackman, J. S. (2020). A psychoanalytic view of reactions to the coronavirus pandemic in China. *American Journal of Psychoanalysis, 80*: 119–132.

Blum, H. P. (1976). Acting out, the psychoanalytic process, and interpretation. *Annual of Psychoanalysis, 4*: 163–184.

Böhm, T. (2002). Reflections on psychoanalytic listening. *Scandinavian Psychoanalytic Review, 25*: 20–26.

Bowlby, J. (1977). *The Making and Breaking of Affectional Bonds*. London: Tavistock.

Boyer, L. B. (1983). *The Regressed Patient*. New York: Jason Aronson.

Boyer, L. B. (1999). *Countertransference and Regression*. Northvale, NJ: Jason Aronson.

Brien, C., O'Connor, J., & Russell-Carroll, D. (2018). "Meaningless carrying-on": A psychoanalytically-oriented qualitative study of compulsive hoarding. *Psychoanalytic Psychology, 35*: 270–279.

Burlingham, D. (1952). *Twins*. New York: International Universities Press.

Cambor, C. G. (1969). Preoedipal factors in superego development: The influence of multiple mothers. *Psychoanalytic Quarterly, 38*: 81–96.

Cameron, N. (1961). Introjection, reprojection, and hallucination in the interaction between schizophrenic patient and therapist. *International Journal of Psychoanalysis, 42*: 86–96.

Camps, F.-D., & Le Bigot, J. (2019). A psychoanalytical approach to Diogenes syndrome. *Psychoanalytic Review, 106*: 207–223.

Chused, J. (1982). The role of analytic neutrality in the use of the child analyst as a new object. *Journal of the American Psychoanalytic Association, 30*: 3–28.

Cooper, A. M. (Ed.) (2006). *Contemporary Psychoanalysis in America: Leading Analysts Present Their Work*. Washington, DC: American Psychiatric Publishing.

De Masi, F. (2019). Essential elements of the work of a supervisor. *American Journal of Psychoanalysis, 79*(3): 388–397.

Eidelberg, L. (1954). *An Outline of Comparative Pathology of Neurosis*. New York: International Universities Press.

Escoll, J. E. (2005). Man's best friend. In: S. Akhtar & V. D. Volkan (Eds.), *Mental Zoo: Animals in the Human Mind and Its Pathology* (pp. 127–159). New York: International Universities Press.

Fenichel, O. (1945). *The Psychoanalytic Theory of Neurosis*. New York: W. W. Norton.

Frawley-O'Dea, M. G., & Sarnat, J. (2001). *The Supervisory Relationship: A Contemporary Supervisory Approach*. New York: Guilford.

Fraiberg, S. (1959). *The Magic Years*. New York: Scribners.

Freud, A. (1954). The widening scope of indications for psychoanalysis. In: *The Writings of Anna Freud, Vol. 4* (pp. 356–376). New York: International Universities Press, 1968.

Freud, A. (1965). *Normality and Pathology in Childhood: The Writings of Anna Freud*. New York: International Universities Press.

Freud, S. (1897). Extracts from the Fliess papers. *S. E., 1*: 177–280. London: Hogarth.

Freud, S. (1898a). Sexuality in the aetiology of the neuroses. *S. E., 3*: 261–285. London: Hogarth.

Freud, S. (1900a). *The Interpretation of Dreams. S. E., 4–5*: 1–626. London: Hogarth.

Freud, S. (1901b). *The Psychopathology of Everyday Life. S. E., 6*: 1–279. London: Hogarth.

Freud, S. (1905e). Fragment of an analysis of a case of hysteria. *S. E., 7*: 1–122. London: Hogarth.

Freud, S. (1907b). Obsessive actions and religious practices. *S. E. tion, 9*: 115–127. London: Hogarth.

Freud, S. (1908b). Character and anal erotism. *S. E., 9*: 167–175. London: Hogarth.

Freud, S. (1909b). Analysis of a phobia in a five-year-old boy. *S. E., 10*: 1–147. London: Hogarth.

Freud, S. (1909d). Notes upon a case of obsessional neurosis. *S. E., 10*: 151–249. London: Hogarth.

Freud, S. (1914g). Remembering, repeating, and working-through (Further recommendations on the technique of psycho-analysis, II). *S. E., 12*: 145–156. London: Hogarth.

Freud, S. (1915a). Observations on transference love (Further recommendations on the technique of psycho-analysis, III). *S. E., 12*: 157–172. London: Hogarth.

Freud, S. (1918b). From the history of an infantile neurosis. *S. E., 17*: 7–122. London: Hogarth.

Freud, S. (1919a). Lines of advances in psycho-analytic therapy. *S. E., 17*: 157–168. London: Hogarth.

Freud, S. (1928b). Dostoevsky and parricide. *S. E., 21*: 175–196. London: Hogarth.

Furman, E. (1974). *A Child's Parent Dies: Studies in Childhood Bereavement*. New Haven, CT: Yale University Press.

Giovacchini, P. L. (1969). The influence of interpretation upon schizophrenic patients. *International Journal of Psychoanalysis, 50*: 179–186.

Giovacchini, P. L. (1972). Interpretation and the definition of the analytic setting. In: P. L. Giovacchini (Ed.), *Tactics and Techniques in Psychoanalytic Therapy, Vol. II* (pp. 5–94). New York: Jason Aronson.

Giugliano, J. R. (2003). Psychoanalytic overview of excessive sexual behavior and addiction. *Sexual Addiction & Compulsivity, 10*: 275–290.

Green, A. (2000). The intrapsychic and the intrasubjective in psychoanalysis. *Psychoanalytic Quarterly, 69*: 1–39.

Greenacre, P. (1952). *Trauma, Growth and Personality.* New York: W. W. Norton.

Hoffer, A. (1985). Towards a definition of neutrality. *Journal of the American Psychoanalytic Association, 31*: 771–795.

Kernberg, O. F. (1970). Factors in the psychoanalytic treatment of narcissistic personalities. *Journal of the American Psychoanalytic Association, 18*: 51–85.

Kernberg, O. F. (1975). *Borderline Conditions and Pathological Narcissism.* New York: Jason Aronson.

Kernberg, O. F. (2001). Recent developments in the technical approaches of English-language psychoanalytic schools. *Psychoanalytic Quarterly, 70*: 519–547.

Klein, M. (1946). Notes on some schizoid mechanisms. *International Journal of Psychoanalysis, 27*: 99–110.

Kohut, H. (1977a). *The Restoration of the Self.* New York: International Universities Press.

Kohut, H. (1977b). Preface – Psychodynamics of drug dependence. *National Institute on Drug Abuse Research Monograph* 12 (pp. vii–ix). Washington, DC: U. S. Department of Health, Education, and Welfare Public Health Service.

Kupfermann, K. (1977). A latency boy's identity as a cat. *Psychoanalytic Study of the Child, 38*: 363–387.

Loewald, H. W. (1960). On the therapeutic action of psychoanalysis. *International Journal of Psychoanalysis, 41*: 16–33.

Loewenstein, R. M. (1951). The problem of interpretation. *Psychoanalytic Quarterly, 20*: 1–14.

Loewenstein, R. M. (1958). Remarks on some variations in psychoanalytic technique. *International Journal of Psychoanalysis, 39*: 202–210.

Mahler, M. S. (1968). *On Human Symbiosis and the Vicissitudes of Individuation.* New York: International Universities Press.

Mansuroğlu, S., & Tambağ, H. (2019). The determination of internet addiction and violence tendency level among adolescents. *International Social Sciences Studies Journal, 5*: 6916–6925.

McGowan, P. O., Sasaki, A., D'Alessio, A. C., Dymov, S., Labonte, B., Szyf, M., Turecki, G., & Meaney, M. J. (2009). Epigenetic regulation of the glucocorticoid receptor in human brain associates with childhood abuse. *Nature Neuroscience, 12*: 342–348.

Moore, B. E., & Fine, B. D. (Eds.) (1990). *Psychoanalytic Terms and Concepts.* New York: American Psychoanalytic Association.

Nágera, H. (1969). The imaginary companion. *Psychoanalytic Study of the Child, 24*: 165–196.

Nardou, R., Lewis, E. M., Rothhaas, R., Xu, R., Yang, A., Boyden, E., & Dölen, G. (2019). Oxytocin-dependent reopening of a social reward learning critical period with MDMA. *Nature, 569*: 116–120.

Nickman, S. L. (1985). Losses in adoption: The need for dialogue. *Psychoanalytic Study of the Child, 40*: 365–398.

Novey, S. (1968). *The Second Look: The Reconstruction of Personal History in Psychiatry and Psychoanalysis.* Baltimore, MD: Johns Hopkins University Press.

Novick, J., & Kelly, K. (1970). Projection and externalization. *Psychoanalytic Study of the Child, 25*: 69–95.

Poland, W. S. (1977). Pilgrimage: Action and tradition in self-analysis. *Journal of the American Psychoanalytic Association, 25*: 399–416.

Rangell, L. (1968). A point of view on acting out. *International Journal of Psychoanalysis, 49*: 195–201.

Rangell, L. (2002). The theory of psychoanalysis: Vicissitudes of its evolution. *Journal of the American Psychoanalytic Association, 50*: 1109–1137.

Rose, G. (1969). Transference birth fantasies and narcissism. *Journal of the American Psychoanalytic Association, 17*: 1015–1029.

Rothstein, A. (1999). Participant in a panel discussion on: Four aspects of the enactment concept: Definitions, therapeutic effects, dangers, history. *Journal of Clinical Psychoanalysis, 8*: 9–61.

Sanford, B. (1966). A patient and her cats. *Psychoanalytic Forum, 1*: 170–176.

Savelle-Rocklin, N., & Akhtar, S. (2019). *Beyond the Primal Addiction: Food, Sex, Gambling, Internet, Shopping, and Work.* New York: Taylor & Francis.

Searles, H. (1960). *The Nonhuman Environment in Normal Development and Schizophrenia.* New York: International Universities Press.

Sethi, S., Lin, H. H ., Shepherd, A. K., Volkan, P. C., Su, C. Y., & Wang, J. W. (2019). Social context enhances hormonal modulation of pheromone detection in Drosophila. *Current Biology, 29*: 3887–3898.

Sherick, I. (1981). The significance of pets for children: Illustrated by a latency-age girl's use of pets in her analysis. *Psychoanalytic Study of the Child, 36*: 193–215.

Smith, L. (1949). *Killers of the Dream*. New York: W. W. Norton.

Sperling, M. (1952). Animal phobias in a two-year-old child. *Psychoanalytic Study of the Child, 7*: 115–125.

Tähkä, V. (1993). *Mind and Its Treatment: A Psychoanalytic Approach*. Madison, CT: International Universities Press.

Volkan, K. (1994). *Dancing Among the Maenads: The Psychology of Compulsive Drug Use*. New York: Peter Lang.

Volkan, K. (2021). Hoarding and animal hoarding: Psychodynamic and transitional aspects. *Psychodynamic Psychiatry, 49*: 24–47.

Volkan, P. C. (2020). Personal communication.

Volkan, V. D. (1976). *Primitive Internalized Object Relations: A Clinical Study of Schizophrenic, Borderline and Narcissistic Patients*. New York: International Universities Press.

Volkan, V. D. (1979). *Cyprus: War and Adaptation: A Psychoanalytic History of Two Ethnic Groups in Conflict*. Charlottesville, VA: University of Virginia Press.

Volkan, V. D. (1981). *Linking Objects and Linking Phenomena: A Study of the Forms, Symptoms, Metapsychology, and Therapy of Complicated Mourning*. New York: International Universities Press.

Volkan, V. D. (1987). *Six Steps in the Treatment of Borderline Personality Organization*. Northvale, NJ: Jason Aronson.

Volkan, V. D. (1995). *The Infantile Psychotic Self: Understanding and Treating Schizophrenic and Other Difficult Patients*. Northvale, NJ: Jason Aronson.

Volkan, V. D. (2005). The cat people revisited. In: S. Akhtar & V. D. Volkan (Eds.), *Mental Zoo: Animals in the Human Mind and Its Pathology* (pp. 265–289). New York: International Universities Press.

Volkan, V. D. (2009). *Fanustaki İnsanlar* (People in Glass Bubbles). S. Erdogan (Trans.). Istanbul, Turkey: Everest.

Volkan, V. D. (2010a). *Psychoanalytic Technique Expanded: A Textbook on Psychoanalytic Treatment*. Istanbul, Turkey: Oa Press.

Volkan, V. D. (2010b). *Divanda Kılıç Dövüşü* (*Swordfight on the Couch*). B. Büyükkal (Trans.). Istanbul, Turkey: Istanbul Bilgi Üniversitesi Yayınları.

Volkan, V. D. (2010c). *Hevosnainen: Psychoanalyyttinen tapausselostu* (The Woman Who Lived with Horses). Helsinki: Therapeia-Säätio.

Volkan, V. D. (2012). *A Psychoanalytic Process from Its Beginning to Its Termination*. Chevy Chase, MD: International Psychotherapy Institute E-Books.

Volkan, V. D. (2014). *Animal Killer: Transmission of War Trauma from One Generation to the Next*. London: Karnac.

Volkan, V. D. (2015). *A Nazi Legacy: A Study of Depositing, Transgenerational Transmission, Dissociation and Remembering through Action*. London: Karnac.

Volkan, V. D. (2019). *Ghosts in the Human Psyche: The Story of a "Muslim Armenian".* Bicester, UK: Phoenix.

Volkan, V. D. (2020). *Large-Group Psychology: Racism, Societal Divisions, Narcissistic Leaders and Who We Are Now.* Bicester, UK: Phoenix.

Volkan, V. D., & Ast, G. (1994). *Spektrum des Narzißmus: Eine klinische Studie des gesunden Narzißmus, des narzißtisch-masochistischen Charakters, der narzißtischen Persönlichkeitsorganisation, des malignen Narzißmus und des erfolgreichen Narzißmus.* Göttingen, Germany: Vandenhoeck & Ruprecht.

Volkan, V. D., & Ast, G. (1997). *Siblings in the Unconscious and Psychopathology.* New York: International Universities Press.

Volkan, V. D., & Fowler, C. (2009). *Searching for a Perfect Woman: The Story of a Complete Psychoanalysis.* New York: Jason Aronson.

Volkan, V. D., & Hawkins, D. R. (1971a). The "fieldwork" method of teaching and learning clinical psychiatry. *Comprehensive Psychiatry, 12*: 103–115.

Volkan, V. D., & Hawkins, D. R. (1971b). Field-work case in teaching of clinical psychiatry. *Psychiatry in Medicine, 2*: 160–176.

Volkan, V. D., & Zintl, E. (1993). *Life after Loss: The Lessons of Grief.* New York: Charles Scribner's Sons.

Wallerstein, R. S. (1988). One psychoanalysis or many? *International Journal of Psychoanalysis, 69*: 5–23.

Wallwork, E. (2005). Ethics in psychoanalysis. In: E. S. Person, A. M. Cooper, & G. O. Gabbard (Eds.), *The Textbook of Psychoanalysis* (pp. 281–297). Washington, DC: American Psychiatric Publishing.

Weaver, I. C., Cervoni, N., Champagne, F. A., D'Alessio, A. C., Sharma, S., Seckl, J. R., Dymov, S., Szyf, M., & Meaney, M. J. (2004). Epigenetic programming by maternal behavior. *Nature Neuroscience, 7*: 847–854.

Wheelis, A. (1950). The place of action in personality change. *Psychiatry: Journal for the Study of Interpersonal Processes, 13*: 135–148.

Winnicott, D. (1945). Primitive emotional development. *International Journal of Psychoanalysis, 26*: 137–143.

Winnicott, D. W. (1971). *Playing and Reality.* New York: Basic Books.

Yerushalmi, H. (2019). Introduction: Supervisory experiences and their context. *American Journal of Psychoanalysis, 79*: 253–264.

Zeligs, M. (1957). Acting in: A contribution to the meaning of some postural attitudes observed during analysis. *Journal of the American Psychoanalytic Association, 5*: 685–706.

Zhao, S., Deanhardt, B., Barlow, G. T., Schleske, P. G., Rossi, A. M., & Volkan, P. C. (2020). Chromatin-based reprogramming of a courtship regulator by concurrent pheromone perception and hormone signaling. *Science Advances, 6*: eaba6913.

Index